Historic Gourd Craft

How to Make Traditional Vessels

C. Angela Mohr

4880 Lower Valley Road Atglen, Pennsylvania 19310

Dedication

To my son, Joey Lasko, who has lived his life around the many gourd projects overtaking our home. On many occasions, he has had to explain to his buddies what a gourd is, what his mom does with them, and why we live the way we do. He is one of my heroes and I consider myself blessed to be his mom.

Other Schiffer Books by Angela Mohr
Making Gourd Ornaments, 978-0-7643-2716-2, $14.95

Other Schiffer Books on Related Subjects
Decorating Gourds, 978-0-7643-1312-6, $14,95

Library of Congress Control Number: 2007938396

Cover Designed by: Bruce Waters
Type set in Zurich BT

ISBN: 978-0-7643-2830-5
Printed in China

Published by Schiffer Publishing Ltd.
4880 Lower Valley Road
Atglen, PA 19310
Phone: (610) 593-1777; Fax: (610) 593-2002
E-mail: Info@schifferbooks.com

In Europe, Schiffer books are distributed by
Bushwood Books
6 Marksbury Ave.
Kew Gardens
Surrey TW9 4JF England
Phone: 44 (0) 20 8392-8585; Fax: 44 (0) 20 8392-9876
E-mail: info@bushwoodbooks.co.uk
Website: www.bushwoodbooks.co.uk
Free postage in the U.K., Europe; air mail at cost.

What's Inside

Introduction

Walking back in time with a gourd—what could be better? By combining simple hand tools and some common sense, you can have fun with making functional gourds that would be at home in history! In this GourdGal book, we explore ideas about interpreting the past with everyday gourd items such as bowls, sewing baskets, water canteens, water dippers, and more. Many bits of information will provide inspiration for historical events and theater projects. Pick your favorite era in history, or Greek tragedy, and make suitable gourd accessories and tools that fit into the drama of the time.

Part One:

Looking at the Past

Growing something unusual in the garden that can also serve a functional purpose is a fascination for many people these days, but what must our ancestors have thought as they grew natural marvels destined to be used daily as part of their household goods and tools? Historical documents such as inventories or diaries do not specifically mention gourd bowls, jars, or canteens, and why would they when the owners would have used a good gourd till it fell apart or rotted from use, then replaced it with the next gourd crop? These are the questions I ask myself when I think about the past and how gourds may have been used.

Thinking about the past and its gourd possibilities is the premise of this book. The strategies used to make historical gourd items reflect my own impressions and research of bygone times when power tools and gourding equipment were not available.

The town where I live hosts a local historical festival every year during which many folks interpret the Colonial to Civil War eras. I demonstrate the production of the gourd items I would have wanted to use had I been alive during those times: bowls, sewing baskets, jars, water canteens, spoons, and scoops.

Using some of the techniques presented here is a good start to making historical and theatrical functional gourds. Also, visit the many online historical websites that speak about the daily lives of populations in particular periods of time. Reference librarians are a fabulous resource when trying to build an array of possibilities. The level of historical authenticity you want to produce will depend on the amount of research you do for the time period you have chosen. No doubt you will develop personal techniques after exploring and learning. I am not an historian or archeologist, but I like gourds and I like having gourd fun! I hope you will too.

Adapting in the Present

Many gourds used as functional household items are named for the traditional purpose their shape suggested: dipper gourds for water dippers at a well and powder horn gourds (now called penguins) as gunpowder receptacles. I like to think the big bushel gourds came in handy as carriers, and named as such, because they were big enough to carry a bushel of grain. True? Perhaps.

When adapting gourds to a functional purpose, consider the needs a person had to fill in their daily lives, for whatever time period you choose. Much like today, people had to eat, had to store stuff, and had to make do when the budget was tight. What would the common folk be privy to in their daily lives? Surely, rural folks would have had access to gourds far more often than urban dwellers. Perhaps poorer folks used gourds more often than the folks 'in the big houses'. Gardeners would have made use of their gourds more than blacksmiths, but blacksmiths might still have had a dipper gourd at the well.

This picture shows my bag o' tricks for demonstrating at an historical event: knives, antlers embedded with darning needles, darning needles, an ice pick, an awl, oyster shells, coarse sand, a leather glove, some cloth, hemp string, broom-corn scrubbies I made, leather shoelaces and scraps.

Equipping for the Job

Tools needed for this kind of gourding depends on the purpose of the functional gourd item and how primitive it needs to look. When I demonstrate at an historical event, I try to mimic what might have been used during the time I am interpreting, but, obviously, I cannot know exactly how something was done.

(Note: Keep in mind gourd dust is highly toxic to nasal and bronchial passages – something we are aware of now that our ancestors may not have known. If you are making items for a play or reenactment, and are working at home, wear a two-canister respirator to protect yourself from gourd dust that may be floating around your work station. At an historical event, limit yourself to low-dust duties and at the very least wear a bandana over the nose and mouth. Forewarned is forearmed!)

You will find your own favorite tools, because no matter what I show and tell, an imaginative gourding enthusiast is going to figure out another way to do something based on what's at hand...and that's as it should be! There is no definitive means to reaching the end result—only the way that works for you. Hunters will have antlers for making a handy tool, but trimmed wooden branches can make swell handles too. A quilt maker will have bits of cloth handy, and if you live near the shore, you will have shells and sand.

What would you have done a long time ago? Would a fisherman's wife buy a new saw to open her gourd, or reach over and grab her husband's filleting knife that works well for the purpose and doesn't cost a dime for the using? Would a seamstress bother to finish the inside of a gourd to make a sewing basket, or use the cloth scraps she already has stashed away on her shelves to line a gourd bowl and hide the bits of debris left behind from a rough gutting job? Go with the basic tools you already have and you will be on your way to developing functional gourds.

Part Two:

Making Carriers

Turning a gourd into a bowl to carry or hold grain, household tidbits, or herbs is going to be the most common bit of work you do since bowls and baskets could have been used for anything from kitchen and gardening utensils to sewing baskets. I make these for use in my own home and, decorated or plain, they not only are fun to use, but are a daily reminder that nature provides more than food and door wreaths.

Go through your gourd pile and select a good 'sitter'—a gourd that can sit stably if left to its own devices. Having a naturally stable gourd makes the efforts pay off when you can avoid an end product that wobbles and tips over. A foot can be added to a wobbler, so do not lose hope if you have to resort to helping along a potential gourd, but get a sitter if you can!

If you do decide to add a foot to a wobbler, understand that it will eventually pop off with hearty wear. A wobbler can also be "flattened" by scraping the bottom to be level. Although this will solve the stability problem, be aware that the leveled area breaks the gourd of the small protection it has against potential moisture damage. Rub the area with candle wax to add a little waterproofing.

Let's get started...

Picture shows two gourds; one with a foot and one with a sanded flat bottom.

Lined Bowls

The decision to completely clean a gourd's interior or not depends on the purpose of the finished gourd. I personally like the rustic look of a cloth-lined gourd bowl meant for darning or other household items. This type of gourd has a cloth sewn to the rim after the big internal debris was scraped and removed. The cloth hides an unfinished interior and ragged rim thus sparing the chore of completely gutting the interior. It is a quick and relatively clean way to get a usable gourd.

Let's make a lined bowl.

Once you have a gourd that suits your purpose and size requirements, soak it in a bucket of water for several minutes. Letting it sit in a good rain serves the same purpose.

I like to use a broomcorn scrubber to scrape off the debris a gourd accumulates while it's dehydrating. They will soften and become ineffective when wet for long periods of time, so you may want to make several. I make scrubbers by cutting a handful of stiff broomcorn off a broom...

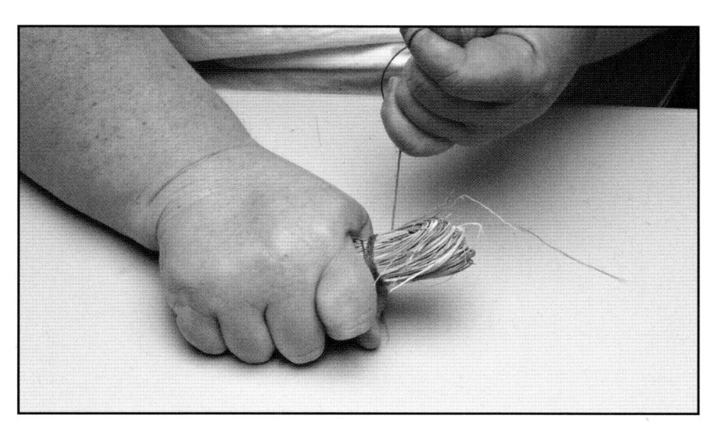

... and folding them in half. Then, tie it together tightly with hemp string by winding the string around the bundle several times. Tie a knot with the ends.

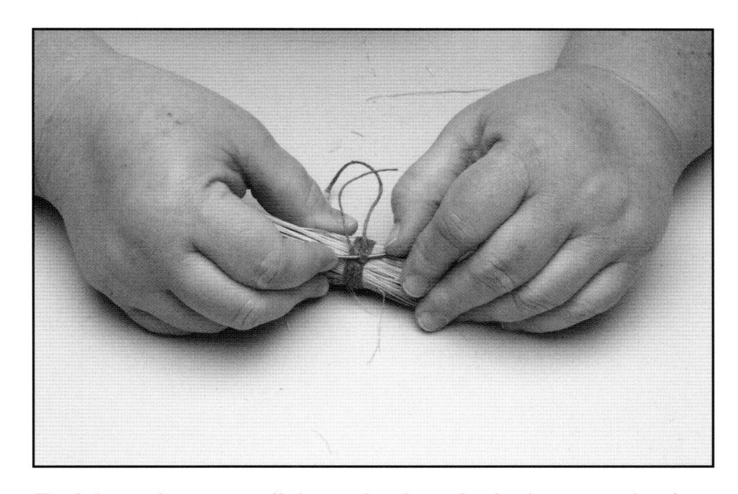

To tighten, insert a nail through a loop in the hemp and twist until it cannot be turned any further.

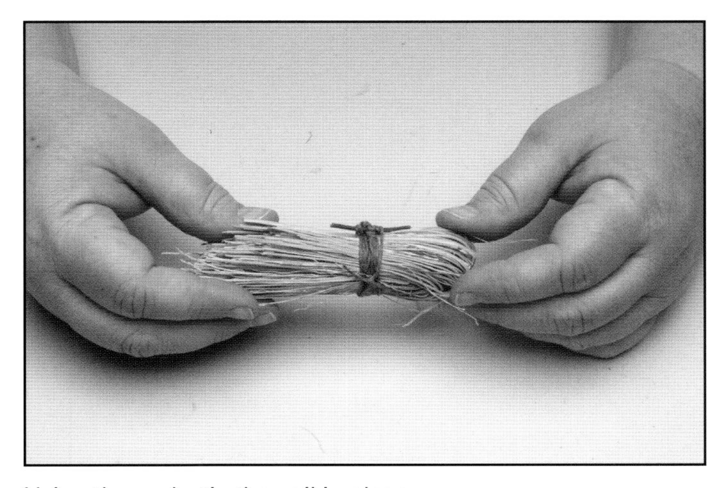

Using the ends, tie the nail in place.

Back to the soaking gourd! Start scrubbing the surface dirt and debris.

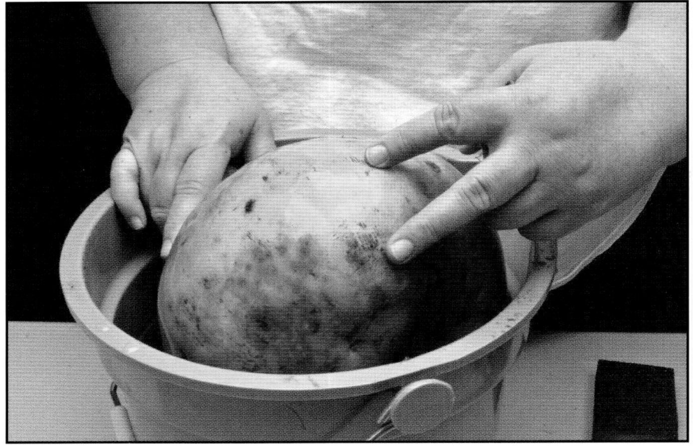

Dip the gourd into the water. This gourd still needs some cleaning. The missed bit of skin or mold makes a ripple on the surface as water runs off.

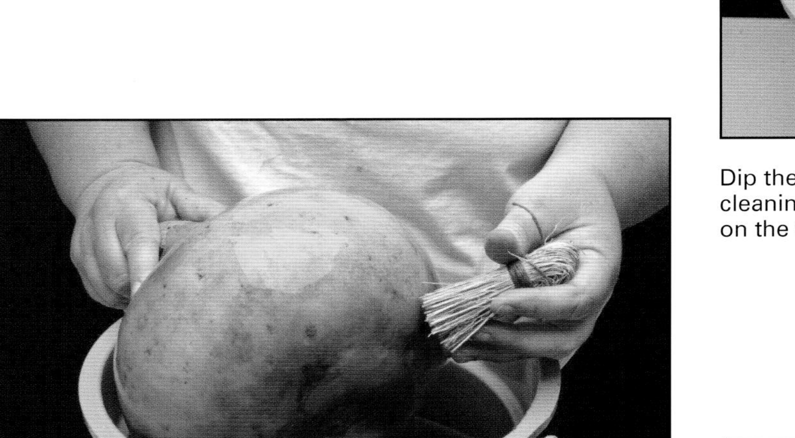

A cleaned gourd surface will have a smooth sheet of water running over it after being dipped in water.

When the debris is gone, the surface will look smooth and perhaps have a mottled color. Mottling indicates where molds grew on the surface while it was dehydrating. It is normal and cannot be cleaned or bleached away. In fact, many folks like this natural look and think it adds to the historical flavor of the finished piece.

Using a knife, puncture an opening or scratch an opening into the gourd by running its edge over the same place repeatedly. (Note: a sharpened flint edge does the same thing.)

Into this opening insert a saw or knife blade and cut around the belly of the gourd.

Take off the top of the gourd.

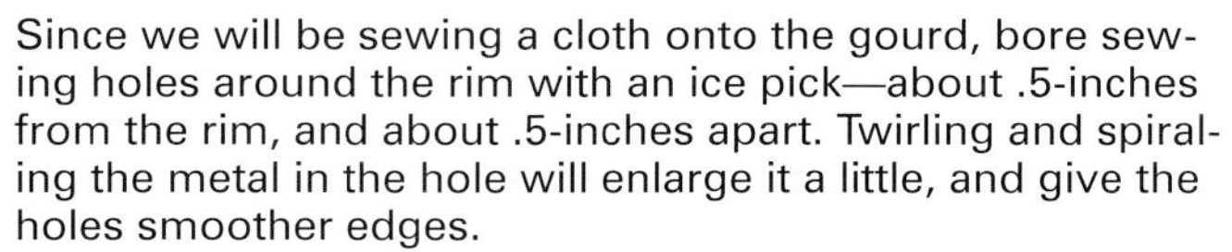

Since we will be sewing a cloth onto the gourd, bore sewing holes around the rim with an ice pick—about .5-inches from the rim, and about .5-inches apart. Twirling and spiraling the metal in the hole will enlarge it a little, and give the holes smoother edges.

Rough scrape the large debris out of the gourd. To do this, I am using an oyster shell.

Mark four places on the rim of the gourd: north, south, east, and west.

Cut a circle of cloth about twice the diameter of the gourd bowl's diameter.

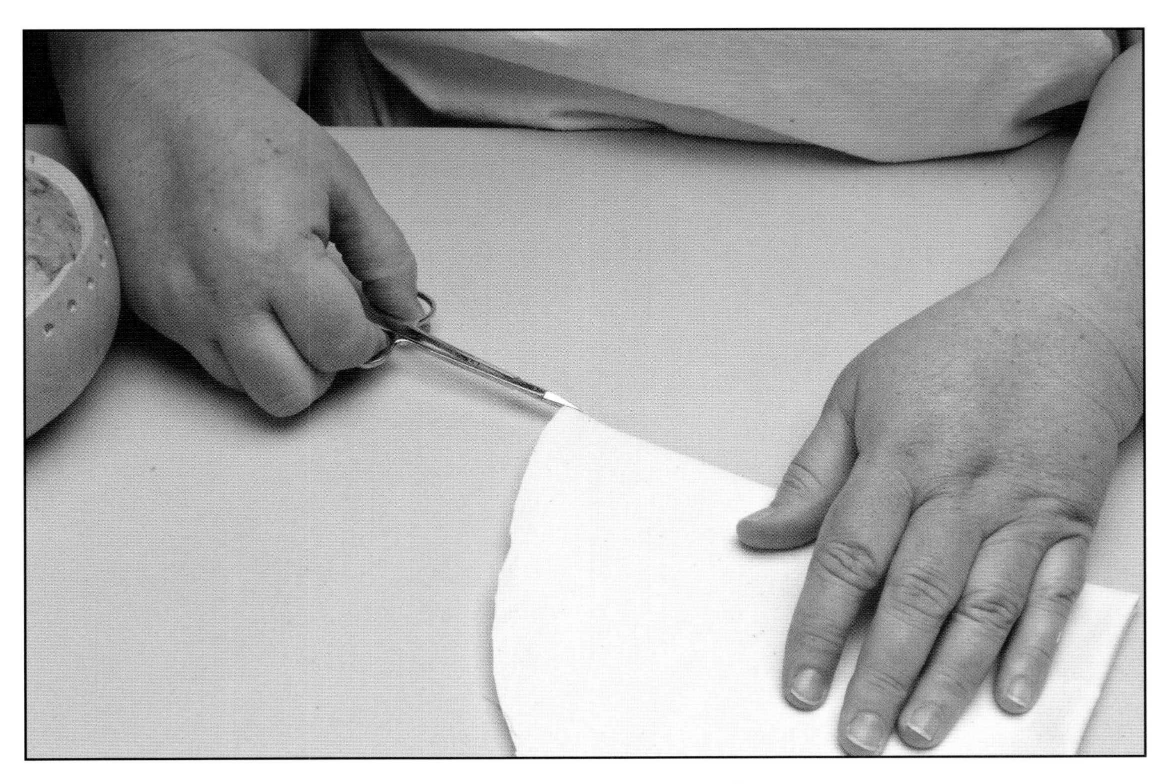

Fold the circle into quarters and snip with scissors at the edge of the creases. These marks will help position the cloth evenly around the gourd's rim when aligned with the compass marks.

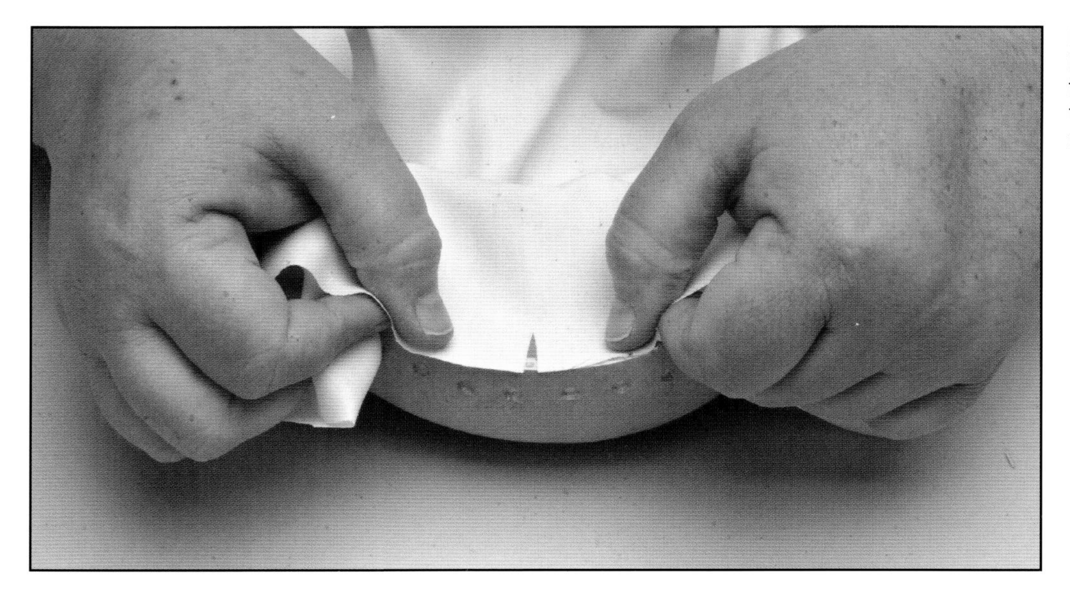

Place the cloth (right side up if you have chosen a printed fabric) into the gourd. Align the cloth marks at the compass marks on the rim.

Stick a needle through the cloth marks and into the hole nearest the compass marks on the gourd's rim. This will not only hold the cloth in place temporarily, it will give you an idea of where the marks are so you can make gathering adjustments as you sew.

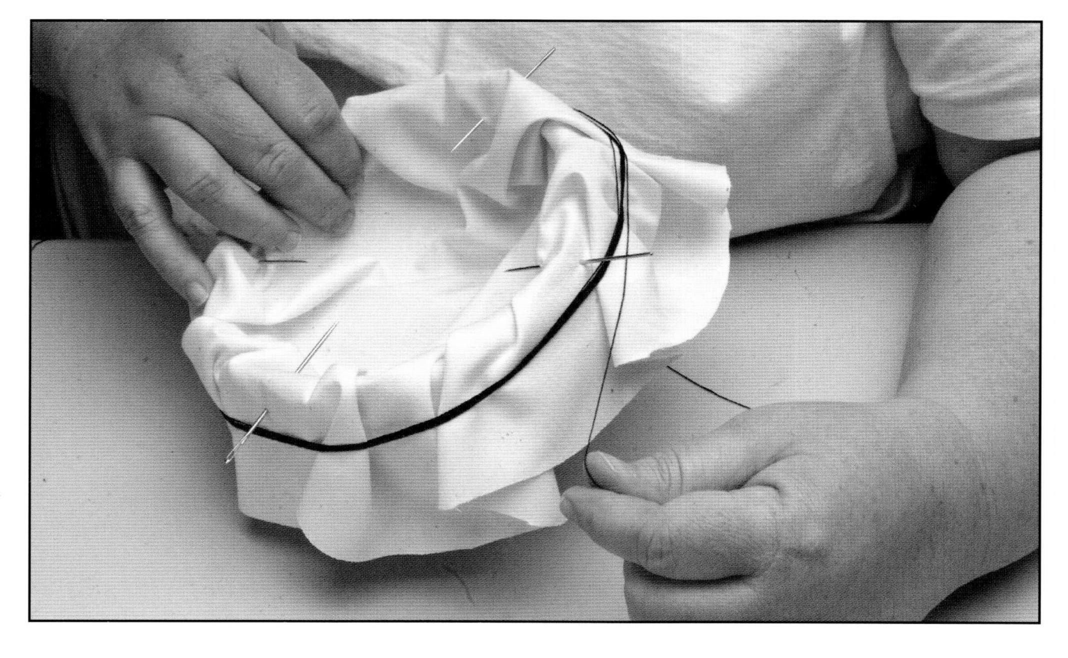

Choose a sturdy thread or string that will fit through your darning needle's eye and wrap it around the belly of the gourd six (or more) times. This should give you adequate sewing material to work all the holes without having to stop, knot, and re-thread.

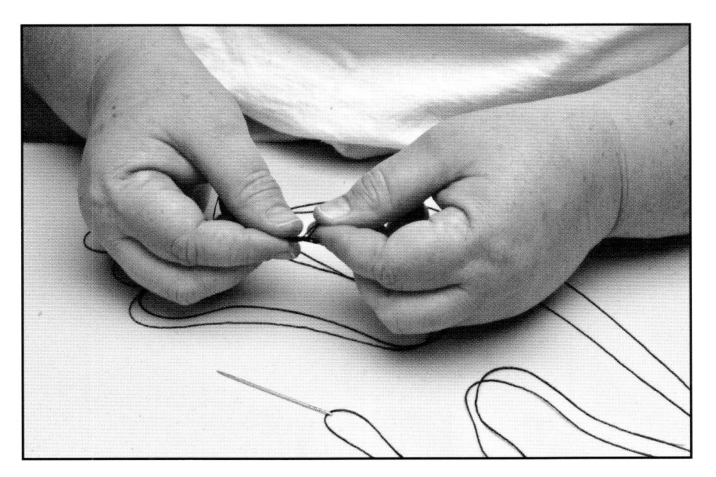

Thread your needle and knot both ends together so you're sewing with a double thread for double strength.

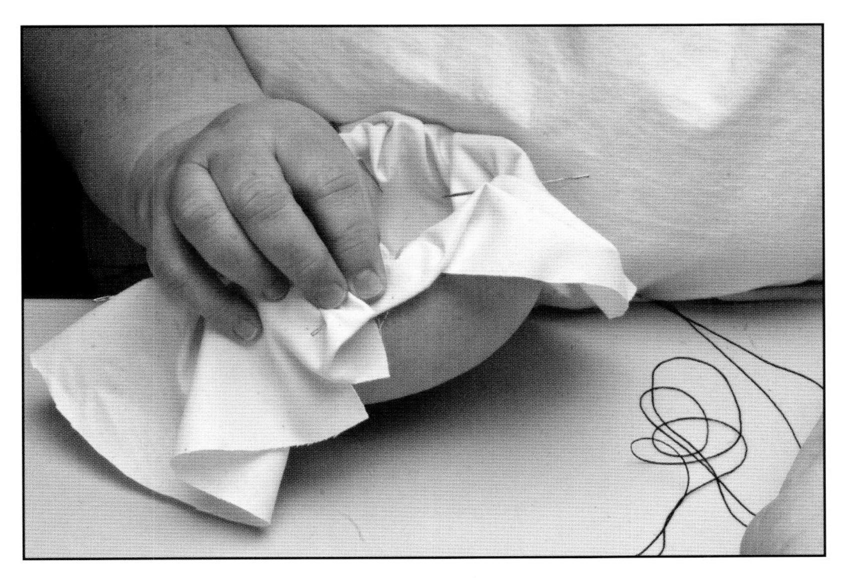

Choose a compass mark to begin, and to one side of it, turn the cloth edge over to make at least a 1-inch hem. Wrap the cloth over the rim of the gourd.

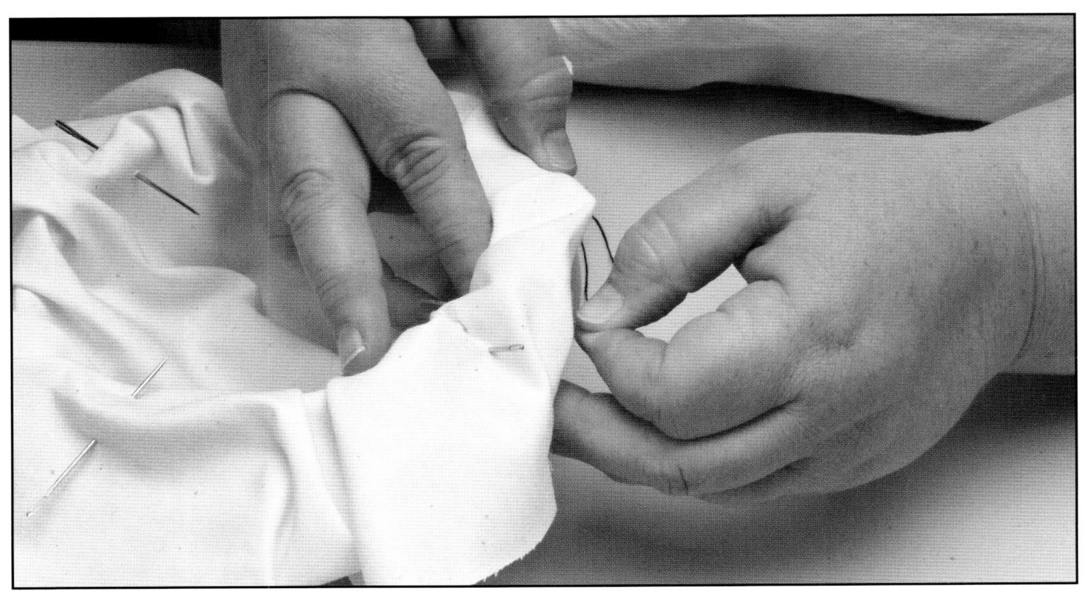

Make the first stitch by passing the needle through a gourd-hole, from the outside to the inside, so the knot is hidden.

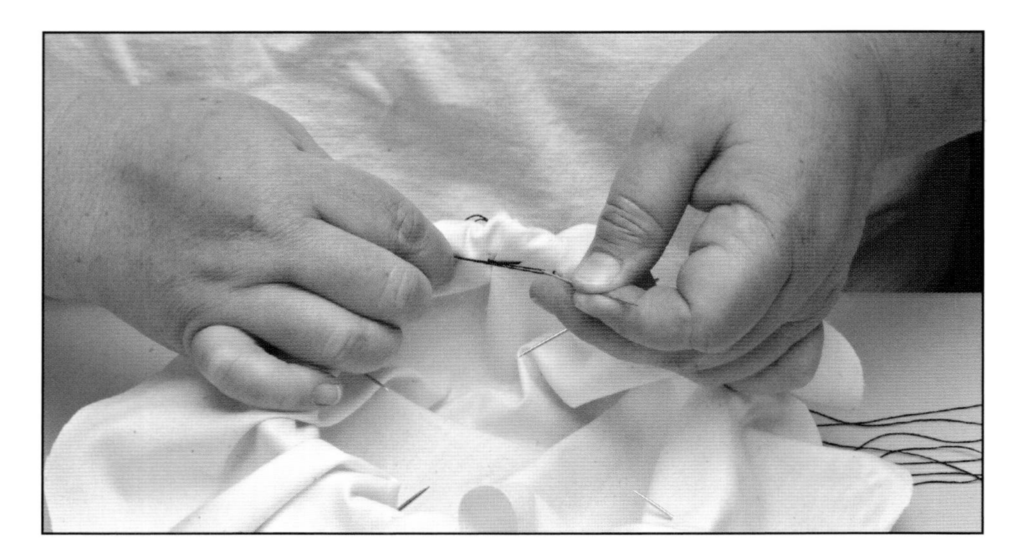

Using an in-and-out sewing rhythm, make a running stitch into and out of the holes you have pre-drilled, going through the cloth as you go.

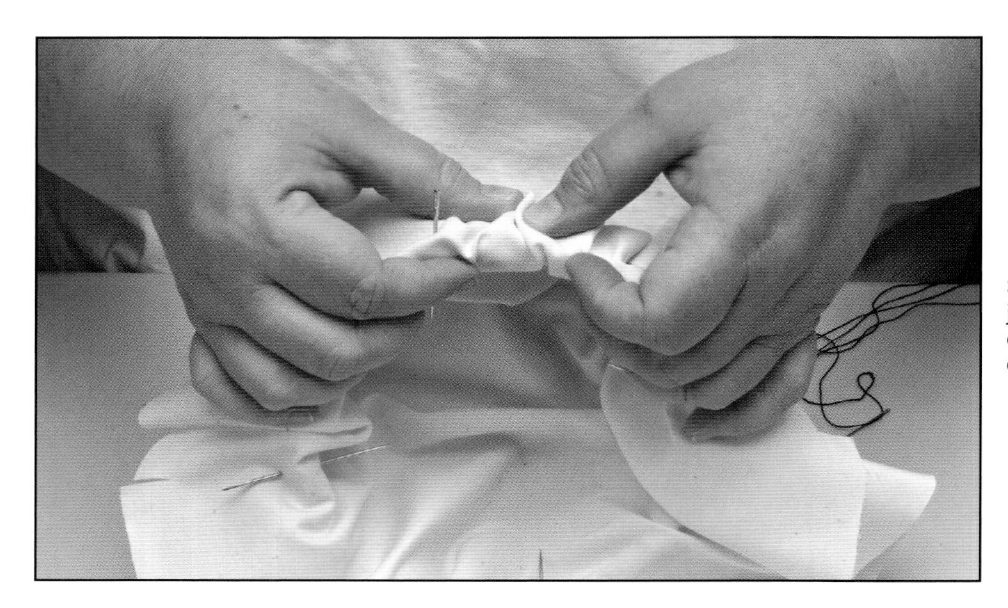

Stop every couple of holes to judge the need for cloth gathering to avoid bunched up cloth at the next set of marks.

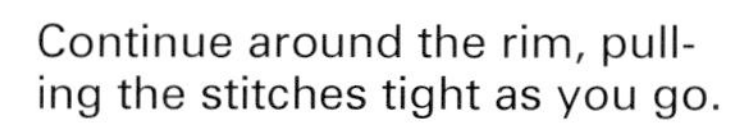

Continue around the rim, pulling the stitches tight as you go.

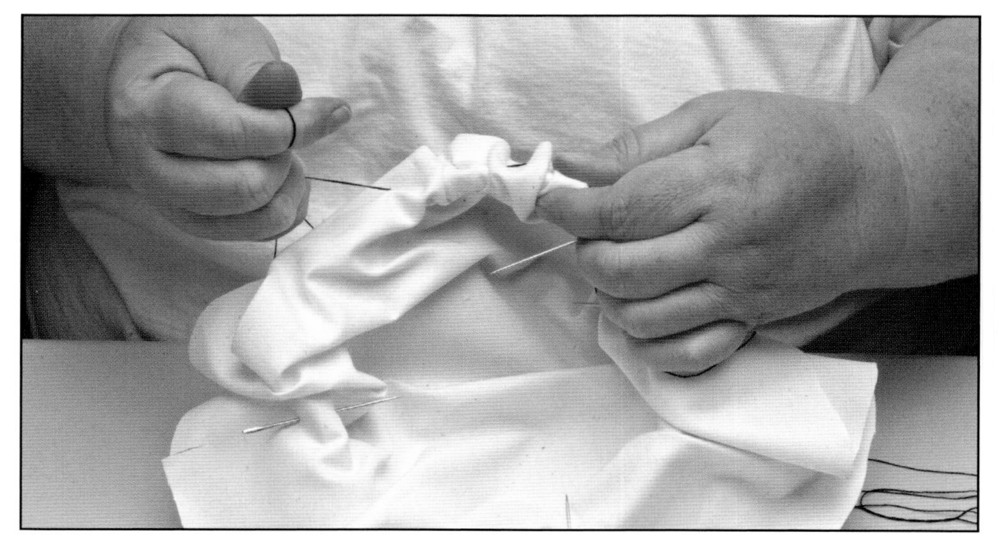

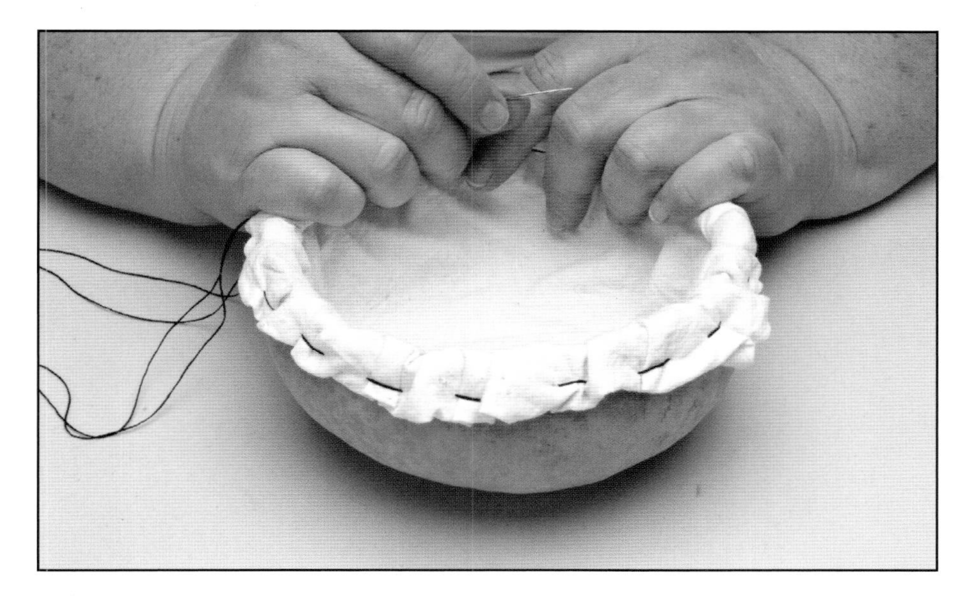

A running stitch will make a line that looks like dashes.

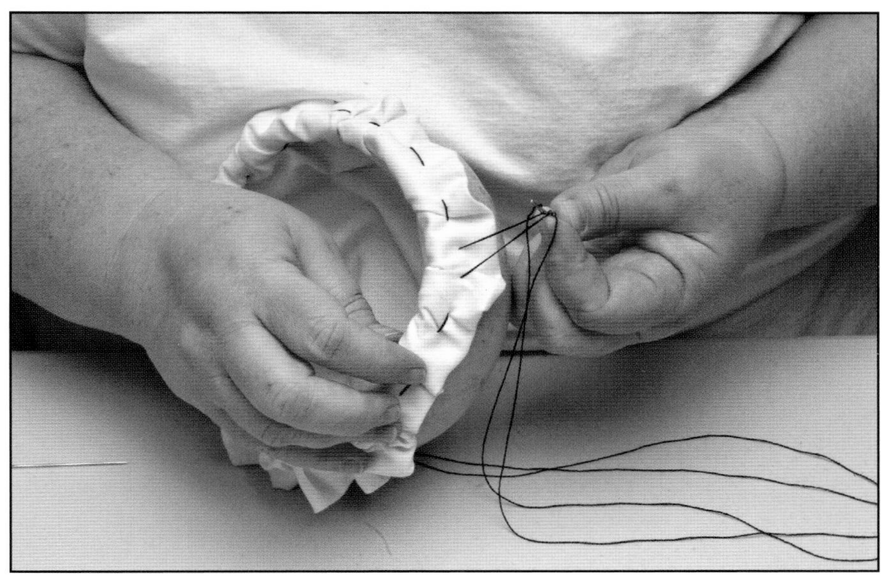

Before you return to the starting point, go back to the first stitch and pull slackness from each stitch all around the rim. No matter how tight you were pulling the stitches all along, there will be several inches of extra thread to tighten.

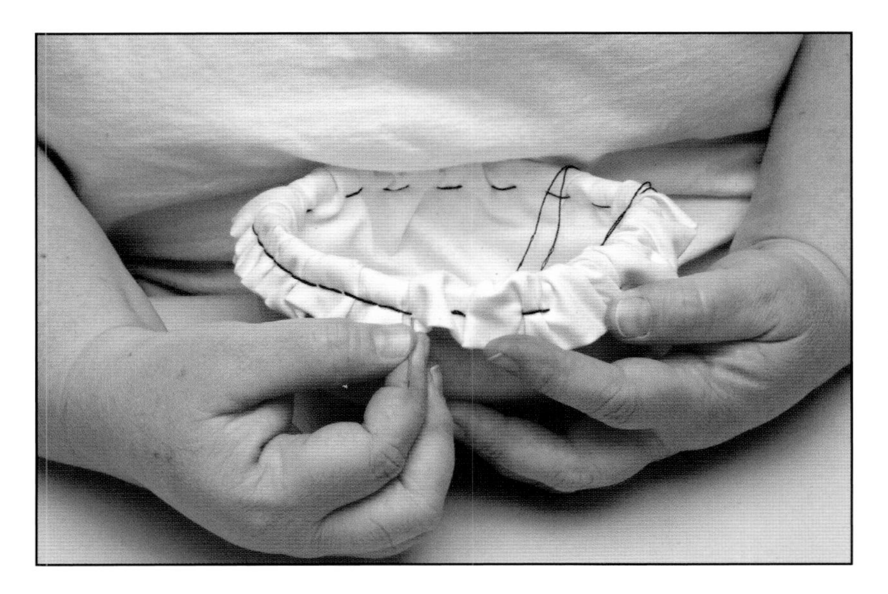

When the thread slack has been tightened, continue the stitches by running the needle through the backside of the first dash. This will start filling in the empty spaces in the line of dashes you've already made.

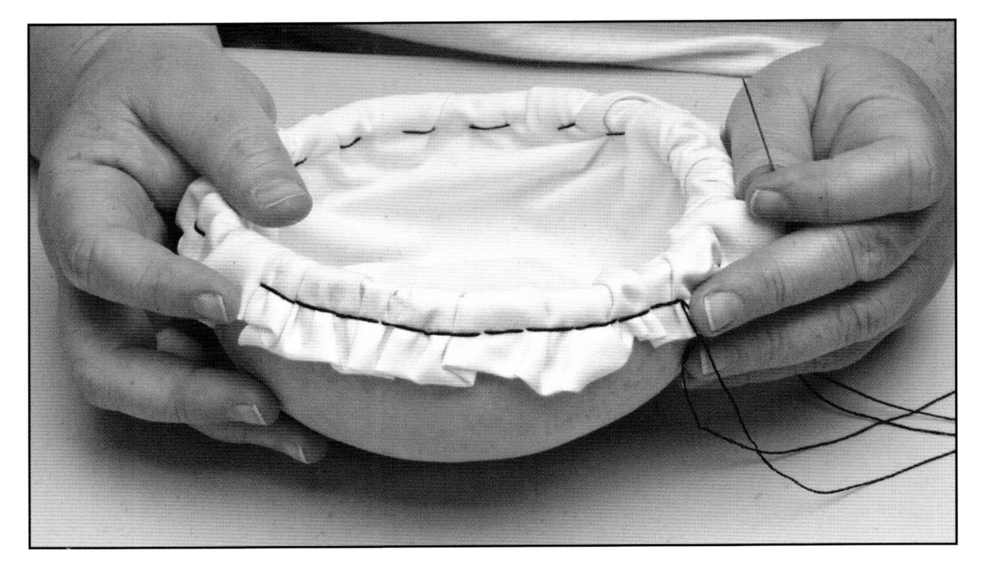

See how the dashes fill in when the sewing goes in and out on the reverse side? It becomes a solid line of stitches.

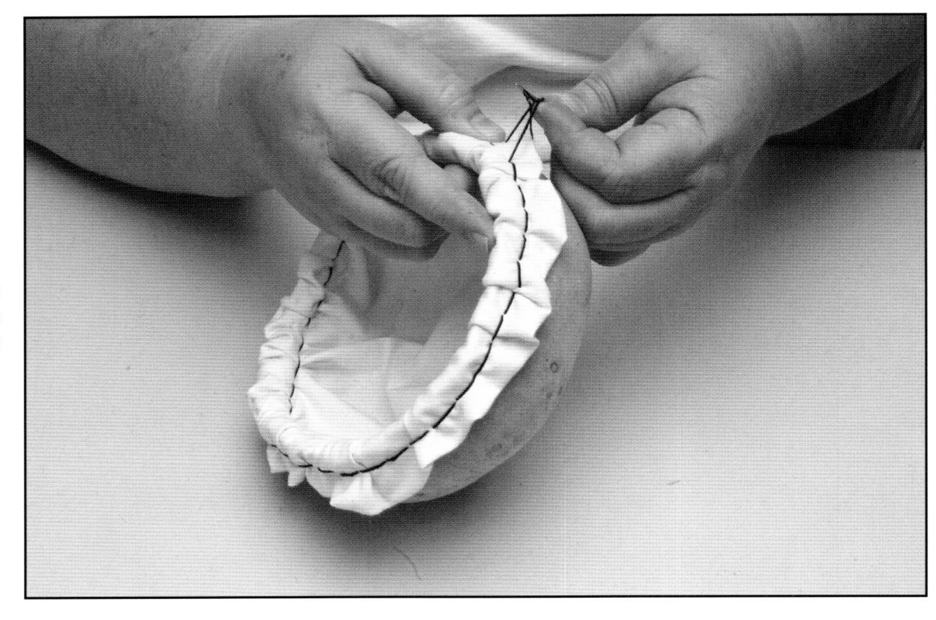

Continue around the rim until you return to the starting point. Check for thread slack as you did for the first trip around the rim.

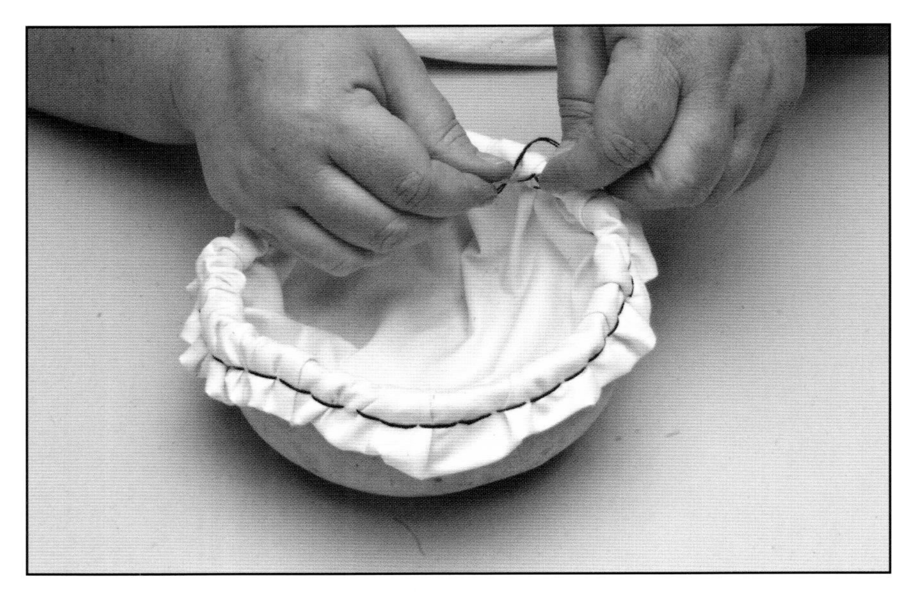

Tie a double knot at the last hole so it is as discreet as possible.

Another old sewing technique is the whipstitch. The needle goes through a hole, up and over the outside of the rim, and into the next hole through the backside.

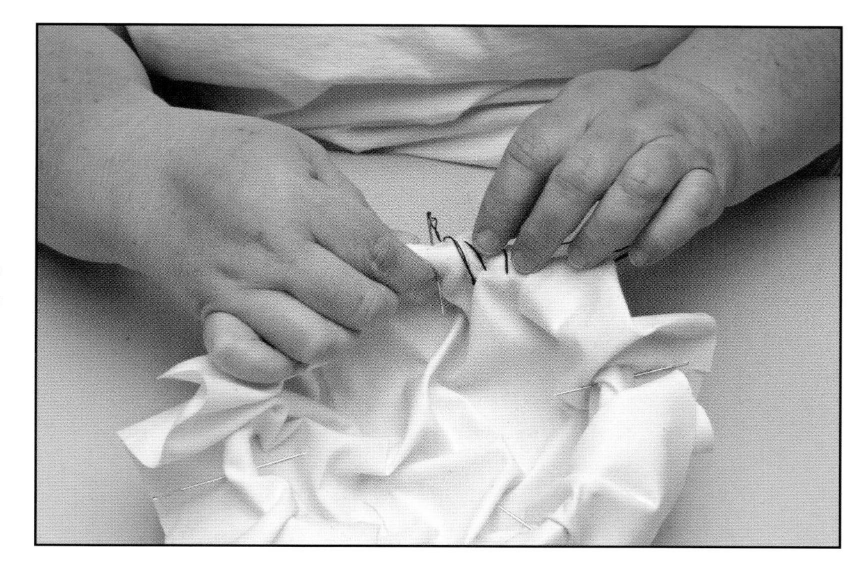

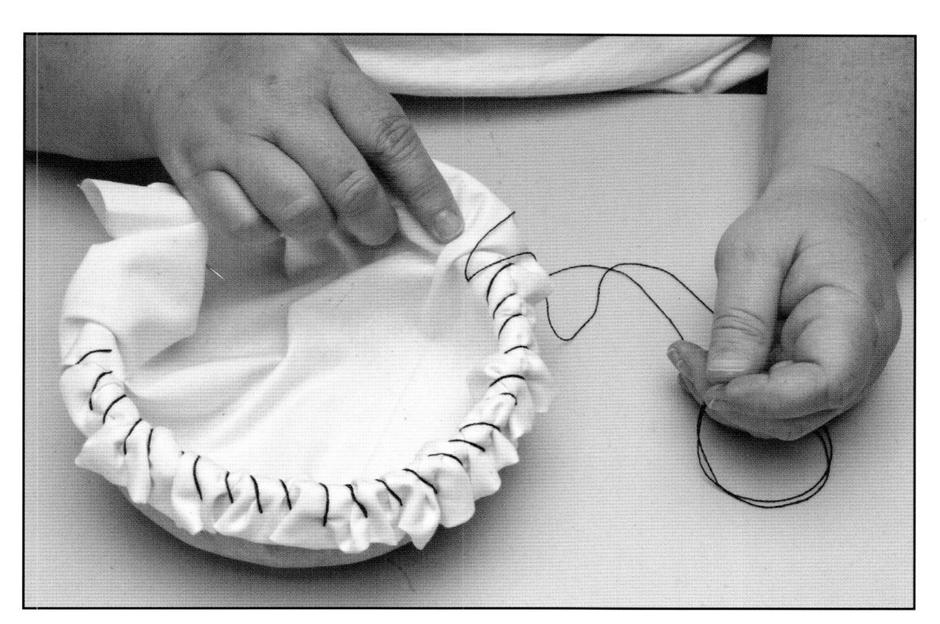

Continue around the rim, gathering cloth between the compass points for an evenly-sewn edge.

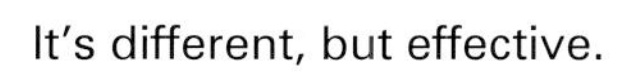

It's different, but effective.

Unlined bowls

On the other hand, unlined gourds are handy for storage, stirring, and measuring. They will need gutting with a finer hand for a smooth interior, but because they are less bulky than the lined gourds, they can fit concentrically into each other when stored—providing the opportunity to have 'sets' of bowls.

Choosing a tool for scraping away the gourd's interior debris can be fun to consider. With a little thought and research, probable scrapers will present themselves: along the shore, shells would have been handy and further inland, sharp stones like shale shards or pieces of metal from the blacksmith might have been used. All civilizations had tools of some kind. See what you can duplicate from what you have in the garage or around the yard.

Let's scrape some bowls!

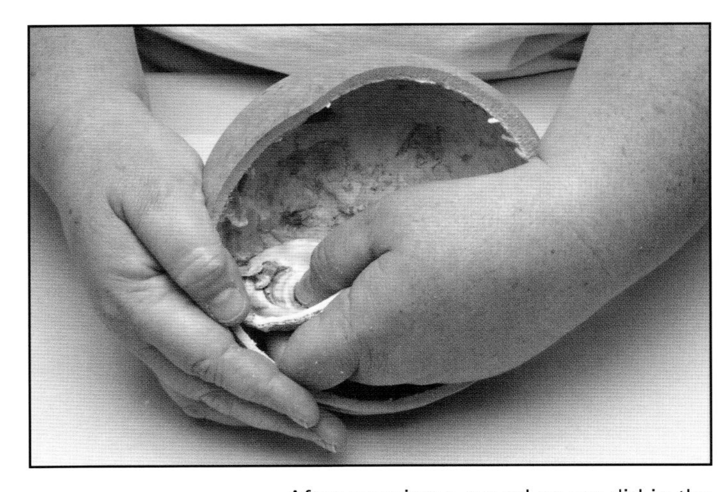

After opening a gourd as we did in the last example, use a shell or metal scrap to finely scrape as much debris out of the gourd's interior as possible. This will be pieces of pith and seeds.

Empty the debris.

Put several handfuls of coarse sand or small sharp stones into the gourd.

Using a leather glove, make a fist and rub the sand against the interior walls of the gourd to release the last bits of debris and smooth the rough spots.

Empty the gourd periodically, refill with fresh sand, and continue rubbing.

When finished, use the broom-corn scrubber to brush loose sand from the gourd.

Once the interior is smooth, turn your attention to the rim. The rim can be evened by whittling it with a sharp knife.

Or, the rim can be rubbed with a rough stone...

...or buffed with the rough side of a piece of leather.

Carrier handles

A basic handle for a gourd could have been just a hole in the side of a gourd. It can't get more basic than that!

Adding handles or straps converts gourd bowls into gourd baskets. No doubt there are endless ways to do handles and straps, and many of you will be innovative on your own. I use leather or cloth because I'm assuming they were naturally available commodities in most households of bygone eras. Consider carefully whether or not you will actually carry things in the gourd because some gourds may not have dense enough walls to support a lot of weight. You will know the thickness of the gourd wall once it is opened; the thicker the wall, the more weight it can support.

Let's make some carrying straps.

To start making carrying straps, choose two strips of leather or cloth that will be long enough to circle the bottom and sides of the gourd and still have enough length to tie in a knot at the top for a handle. Shown are 3x4-inches of canvas cloth, folded it in half lengthwise for added strength.

This picture shows a rectangular hole in the bushel gourd.

Test the length of your straps by sitting the gourd in the middle of the straps and holding up the ends to see if you have enough length to tie a knot for a handle above the gourd.

Remove the gourd for now and lay the strips on a flat surface in a flattened "X" shape and make a stitch at the intersection with a needle and thread to hold them together.

To determine the position of the handle's holes, place your fingertips on opposite sides of the gourd at the area of the belly just before it begins to get rounded. Lift the gourd with your fingertips and see if it hangs level. If the gourd tilts, reposition your fingertips until it's balanced.

Once balanced, mark the spots (where your fingertips were) by collecting soot on the back of a spoon from a candle flame...

Then, use your fingertips to smudge little marks at the balancing spots.

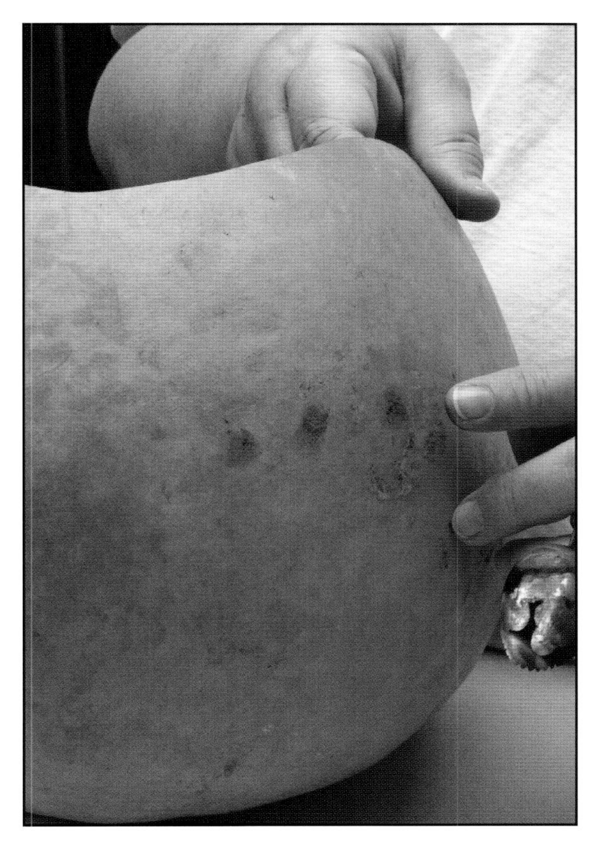

Mark for the handle's holes: 1-inch on either side of the fingertip spot.

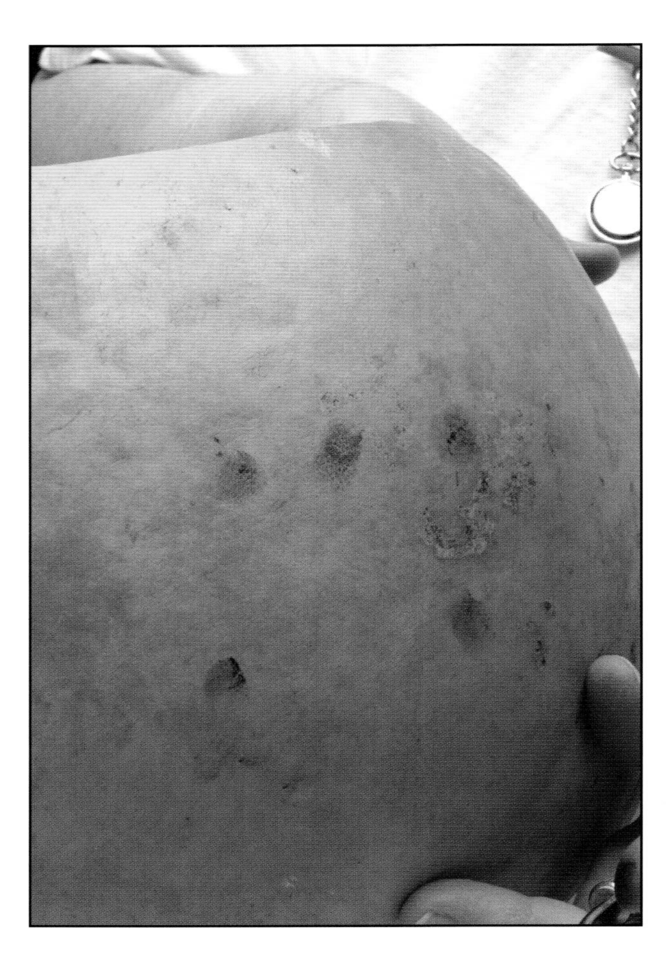

Mark another set of handle holes 2 inches below the first two. These additional holes will help distribute the weight of the objects carried inside the gourd.
(Note: The larger the gourd, the farther apart the holes will be to evenly distribute weight.)

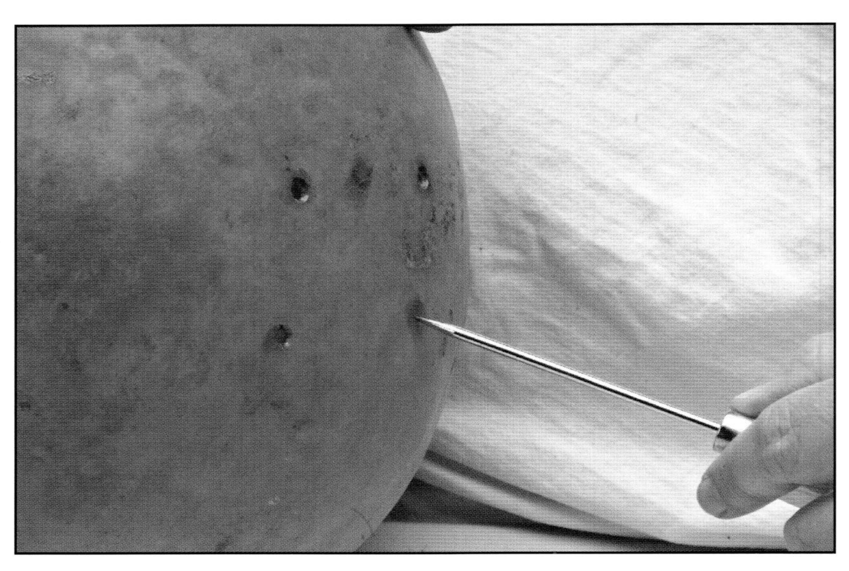

Bore the holes with an ice pick.

Once the initial holes are made, use something bigger to expand and enlarge them for threading the strips of cloth, such as a knife tip. Twirling a knife will enlarge the holes. Try to take away only a little of the gourd's wall at a time because a big chunk taken at once will crack the gourd from the hole to the rim.

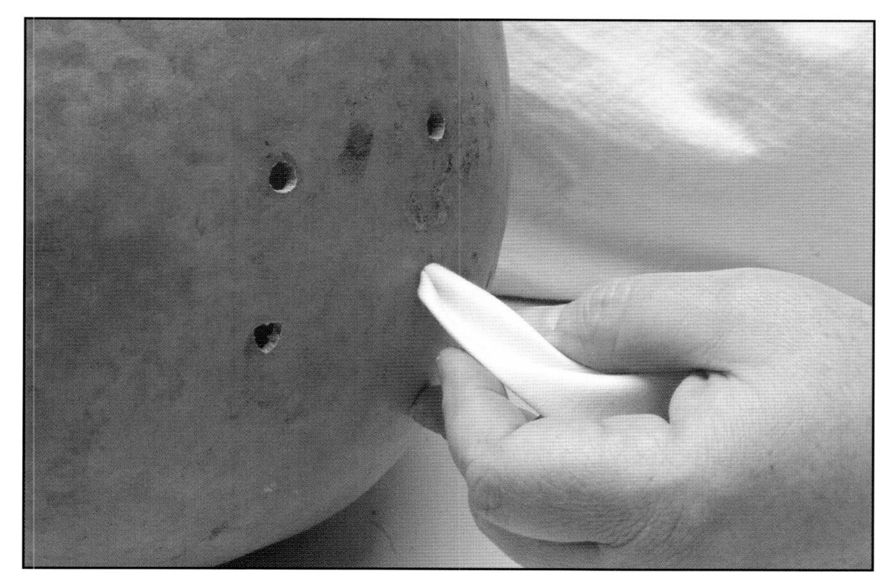

Test the cloth in the holes as you work until you have a nice snug fit, not tight or stressful.

When the holes are ready, get your straps in place on a flat surface and sit the gourd in the middle of the "X" intersection.

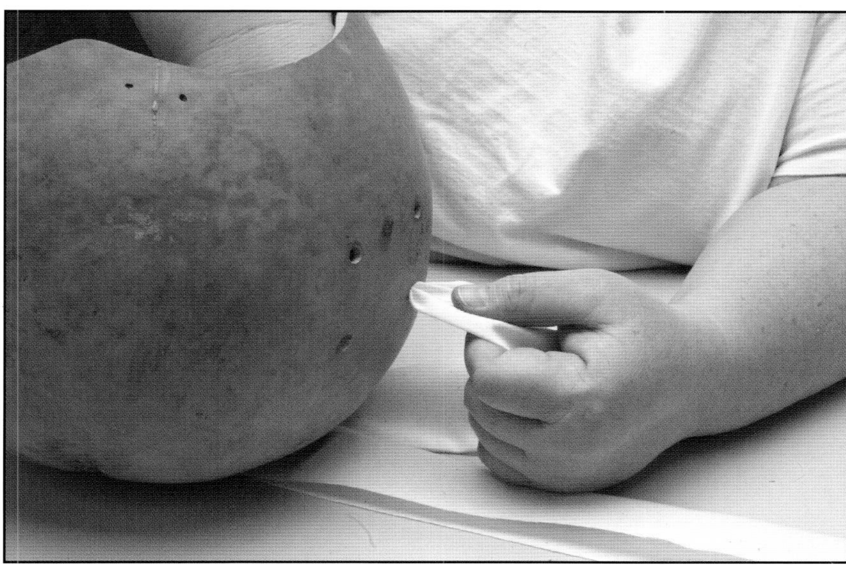

Beginning on one side of the gourd, thread one piece of cloth into a bottom hole.

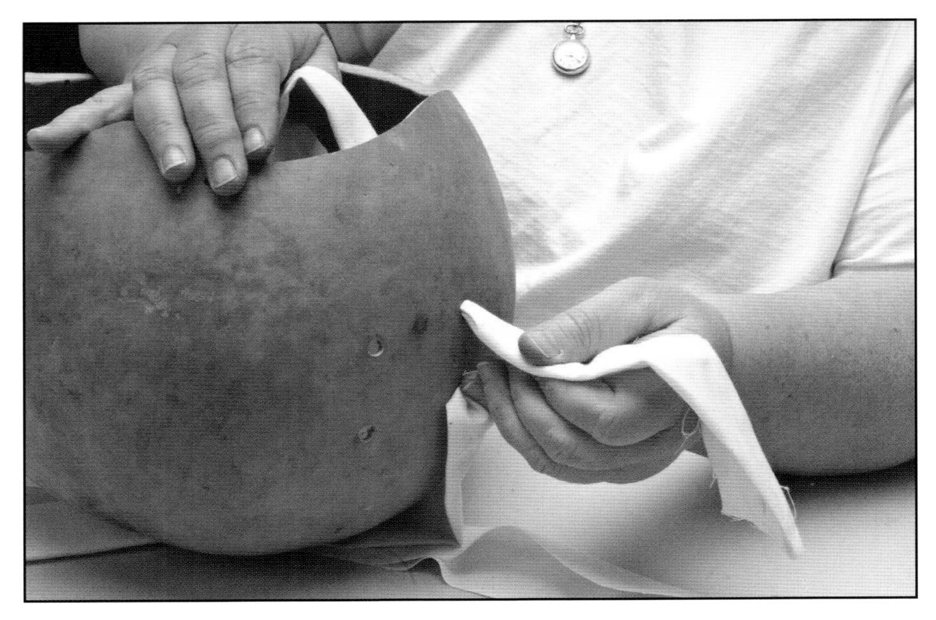

Continue from the inside into the top hole, to the outside.

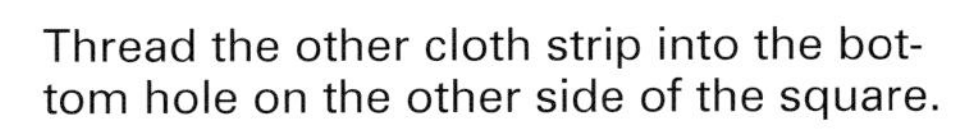

Thread the other cloth strip into the bottom hole on the other side of the square.

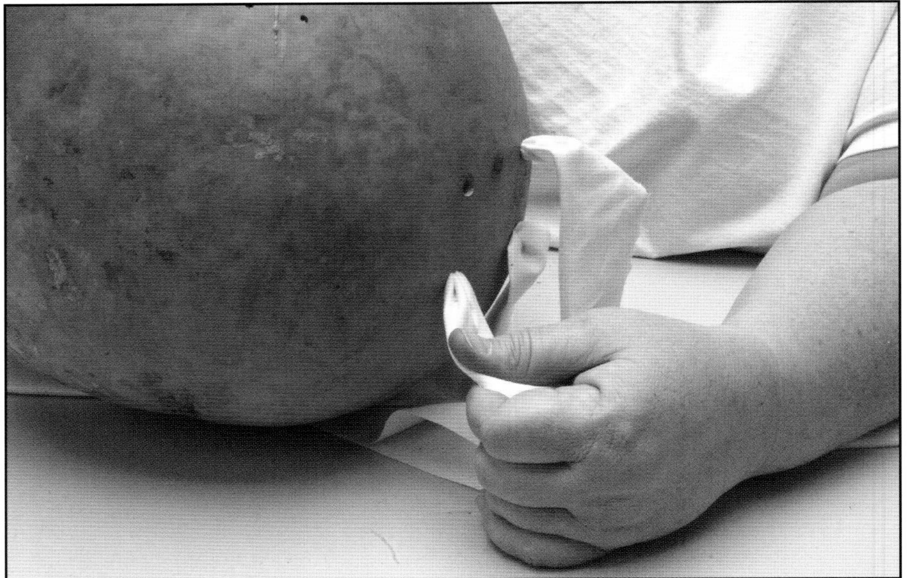

Continue from the inside into the top hole, to the outside.

Do the same procedure on the opposite side of the gourd.

Hold up the cloth's ends and see if they are even or need adjusting.

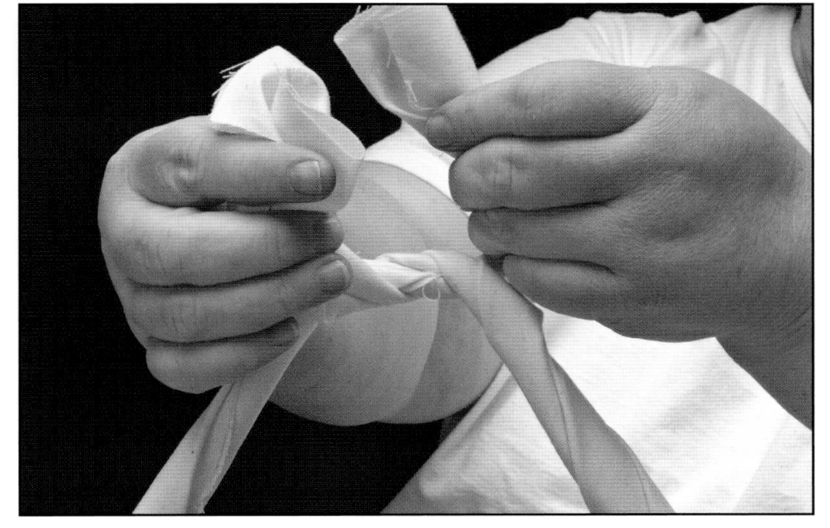

Tie the ends into a knot.

Part Three:

Making Containers

I define a container as something with a lid or needing a stopper: a jar or a water vessel. Historically speaking, gourd jars or vessels have to be taken with a grain of salt, because it is anyone's guess how prevalent they were. I can only assume that if I were growing gourds and needed containers for storage, I would choose to use what was handy and somewhat durable. (And frankly, wouldn't it be fun to use a rustic collection of gourd jars and canteens?)

Use a knife to scrape a line around the gourd just above widest part of the belly so it has a slow wave on the side...

Jars

When choosing a gourd for a jar, select a sturdy gourd that sits solidly without wobbling. A gourd jar needs to be a good sitter, one with a flat bottom. A water vessel is either hung or carried on the body so stable sitting will not be a requirement when we get to that point.

Let's make the gourd jar.

...comes to a pointed notch in the front ...

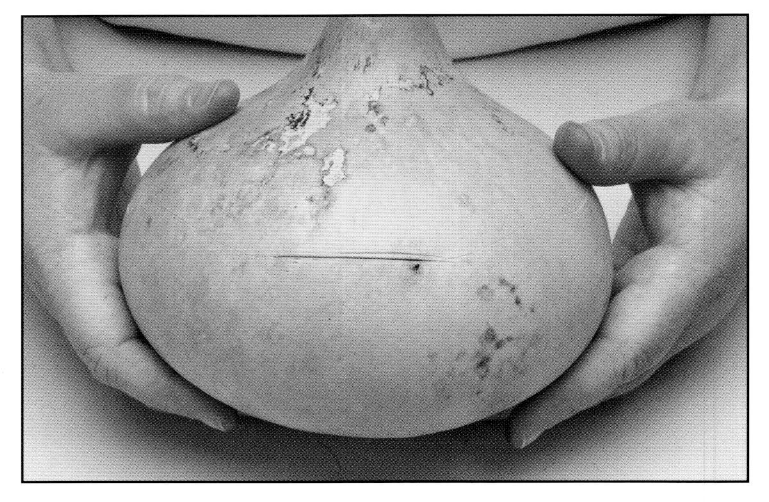

...and has a straight area at the back where the hinge will be placed.

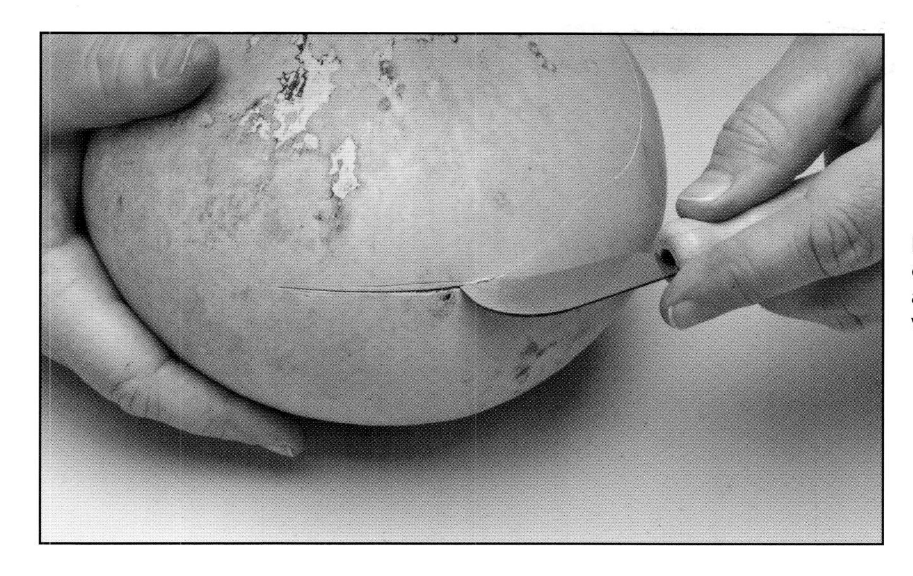

Insert a knife on the straight part of the line by scraping the knife tip against the surface until it works its way into the gourd.

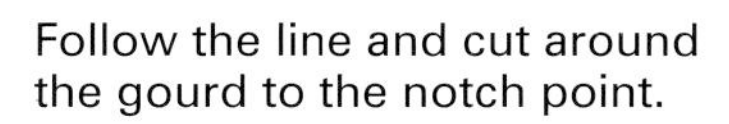

Follow the line and cut around the gourd to the notch point.

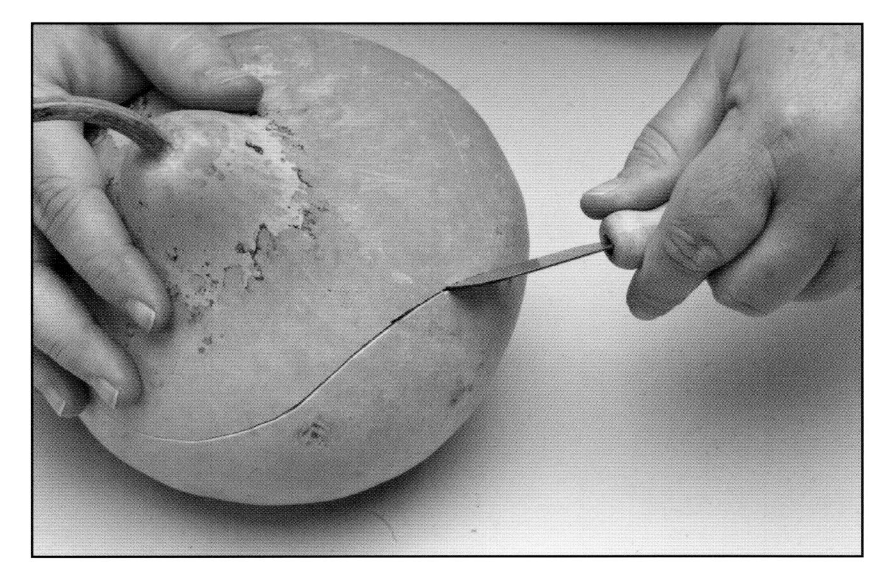

Stop at the notch point and pull out the knife.

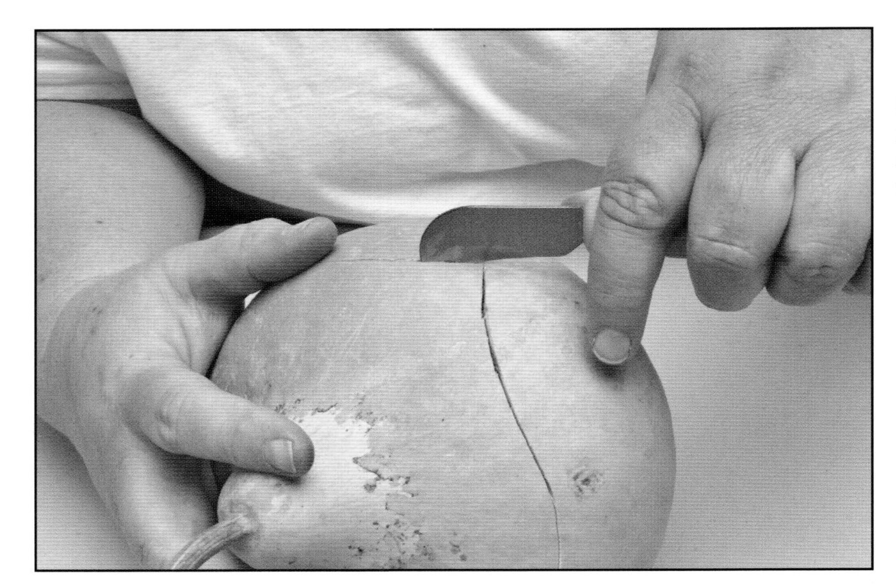

Go back to the beginning, and start cutting in the opposite direction to reach the notch point from the opposite direction.

Open the gourd and empty the seeds and pith.

Gut the gourd as we did earlier with the carriers.

Remember to gut the lid as well.

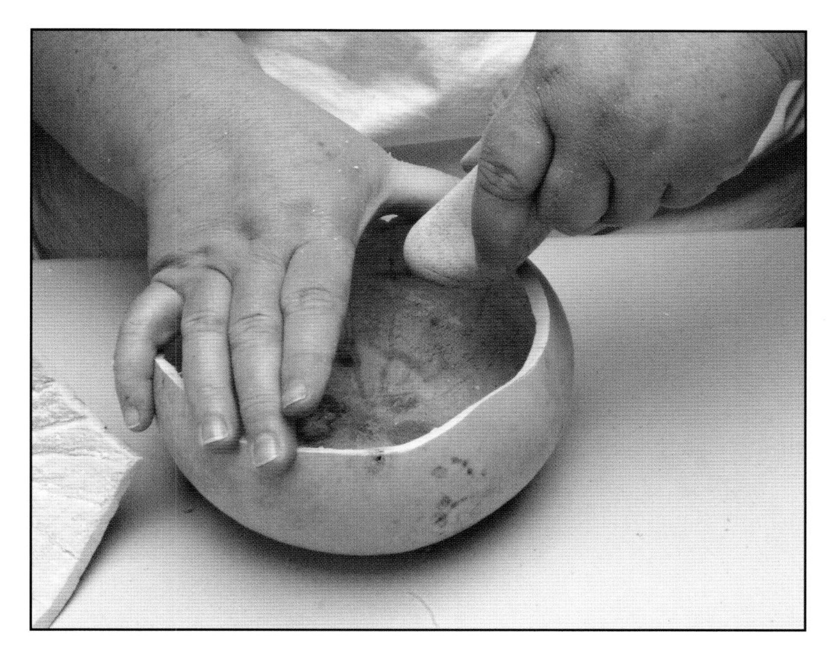

Rub a rough leather or stone along the rims to smooth the saw or knife marks.

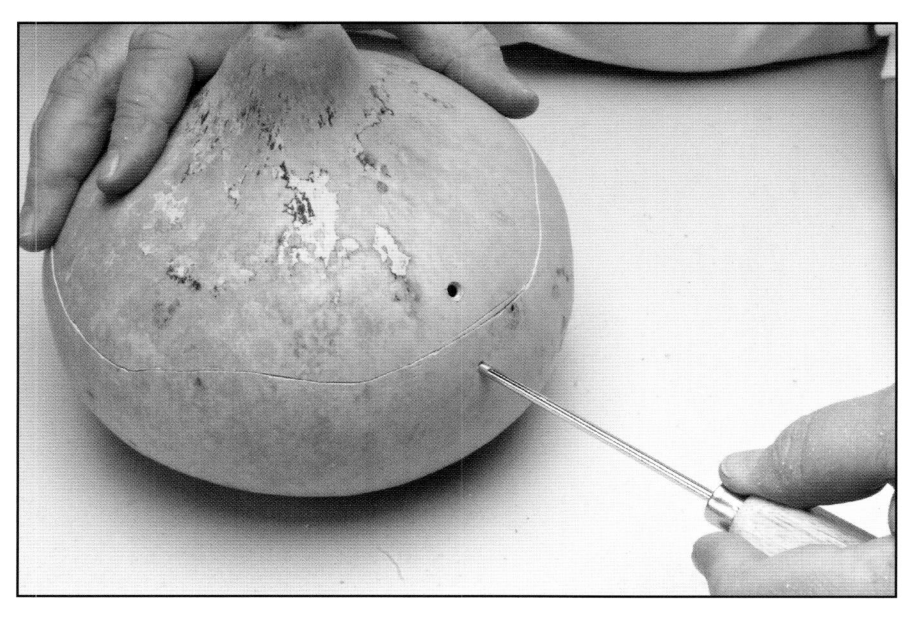

When the gourd is gutted to your satisfaction, place the lid on the belly. At the opening area where the line was straight, bore two holes big enough to thread a leather strip: one hole .5-inches above and one hole .5-inches below the line.

One way to make a basic hinge is to thread a piece of leather through the holes from the outside, and knot the ends against the gourd's interior.

Another option is to bore two holes .5-inches above and below the rim at the straightest part of the original line.

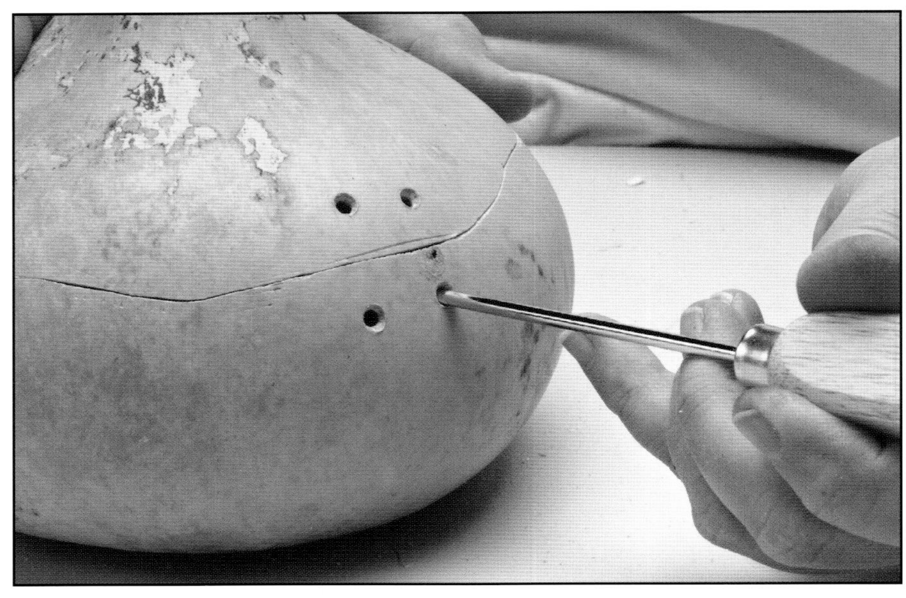

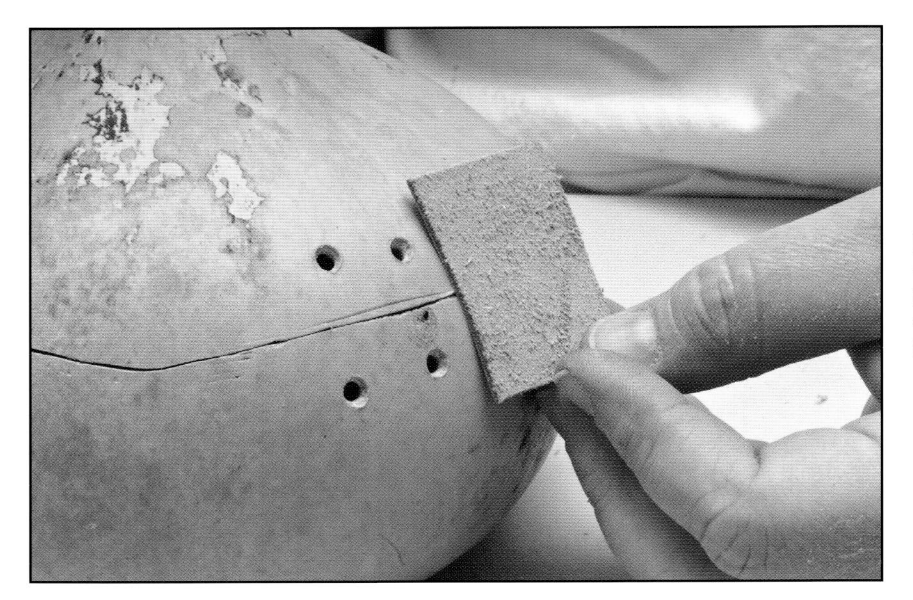

For the hinge, cut a rectangular piece of stiff leather that extends at least .25-inches beyond the holes. The stiffness of the leather keeps the lid from wavering sideways on the rim.

Put a spoon against a candle flame and gather some soot.

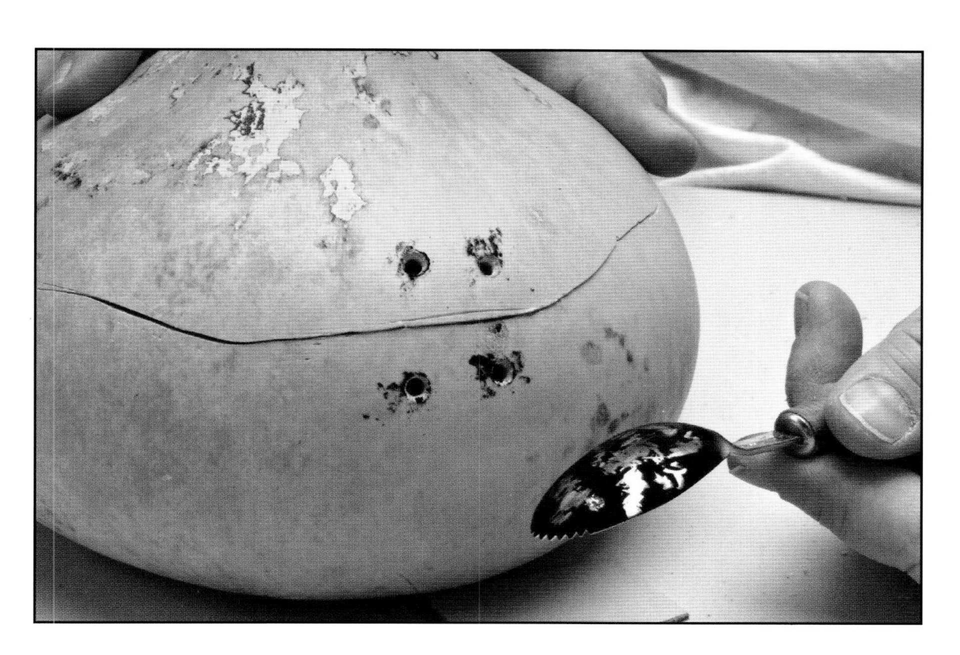

Scrape soot around the holes in the lid.

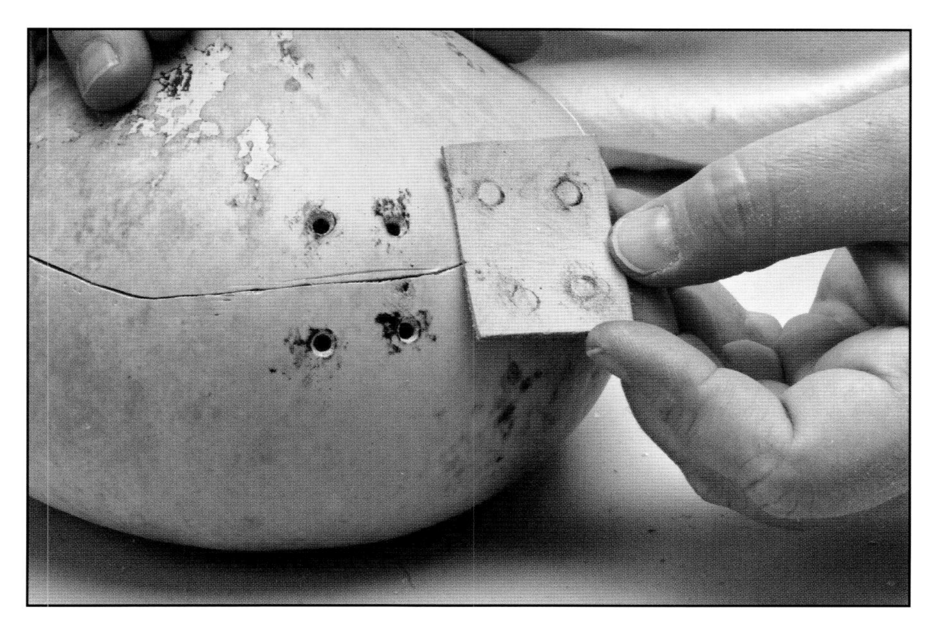

This way, when you press the leathered hinge against the lid, the puncture area for the corresponding holes will be marked with soot.

Puncture the leathered hinge at the marked spots with an ice pick.

Thread pieces of leather shoelace through the corresponding hinge and gourd holes and knot tightly at both ends.

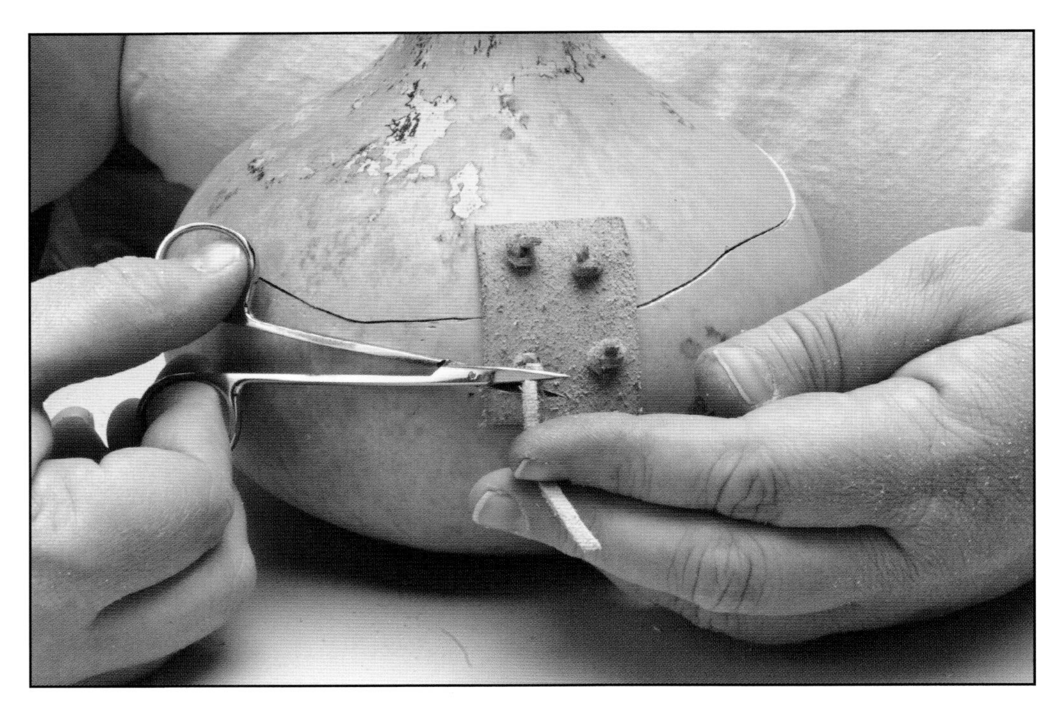

Trim the leather ends.

At the notch on the other side of the gourd jar, bore a hole a .5-inch above the gourd's rim.

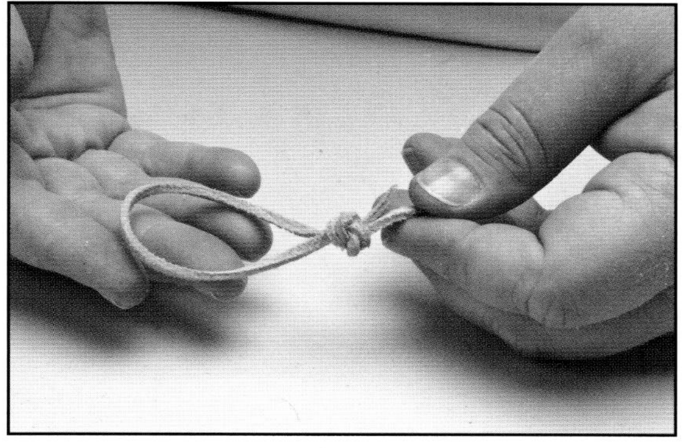

Cut a length of leather that is long enough to make a loop by doubling it and tying a knot.

Thread the loop through the hole, from the inside to the outside, and tie another knot close to the hole, leaving the length to use as a handle to open the lid.

Latches are handy for closing a lid and not having it pop open. The contents are more secure when storing or moving if there are three or four latches evenly spaced around the gourd's rim.

Let's put some latches on a gourd.

Start by cutting three 1x2-inches rectangular pieces of leather — these will be called latches.

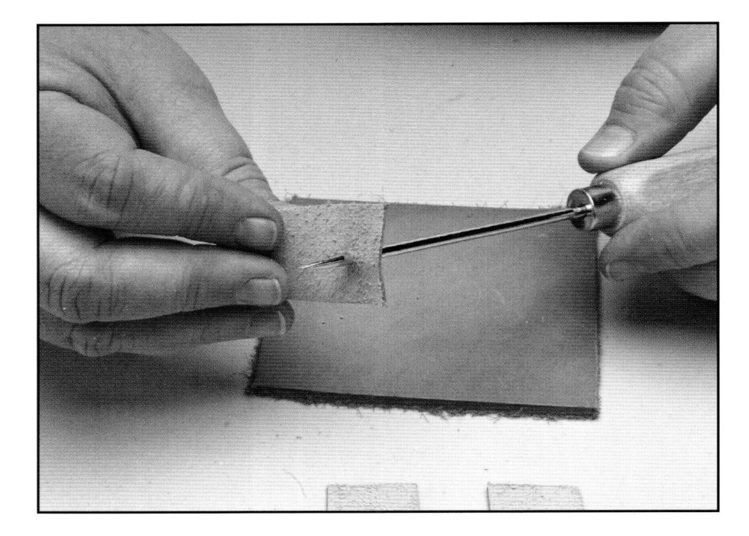

To make the first one, puncture a hole into one end of the latch with an ice pick.

Cut a 1-inch slit into the other end with a knife.

Use candle soot to mark the back of both the hole and the slit on the latch.

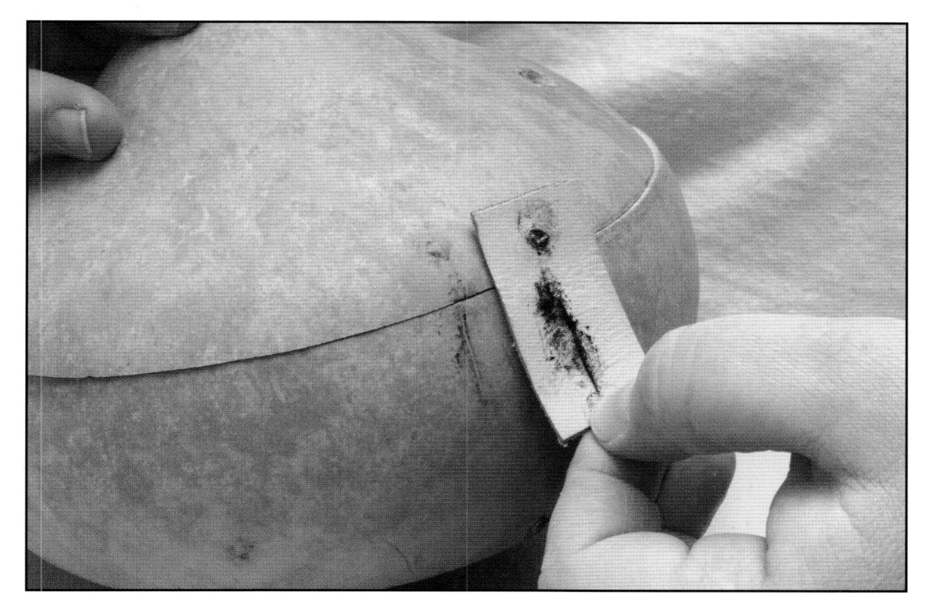

Press the latch on the lidded gourd over the rim seam so that the soot marks the corresponding spots for a hole on the lid and a hole on the belly.

Bore the lid hole.

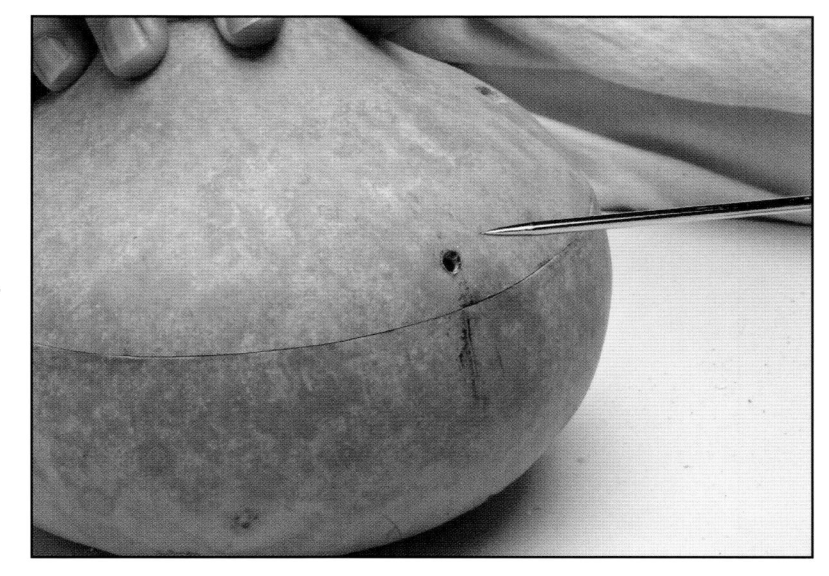

Knot one end of a leather shoelace. Then thread it from the inside of the lid through the gourd hole, and then through the leathered latch to the outside.

Pull the shoelace tightly and knot it against the leathered latch on the gourd's wall.

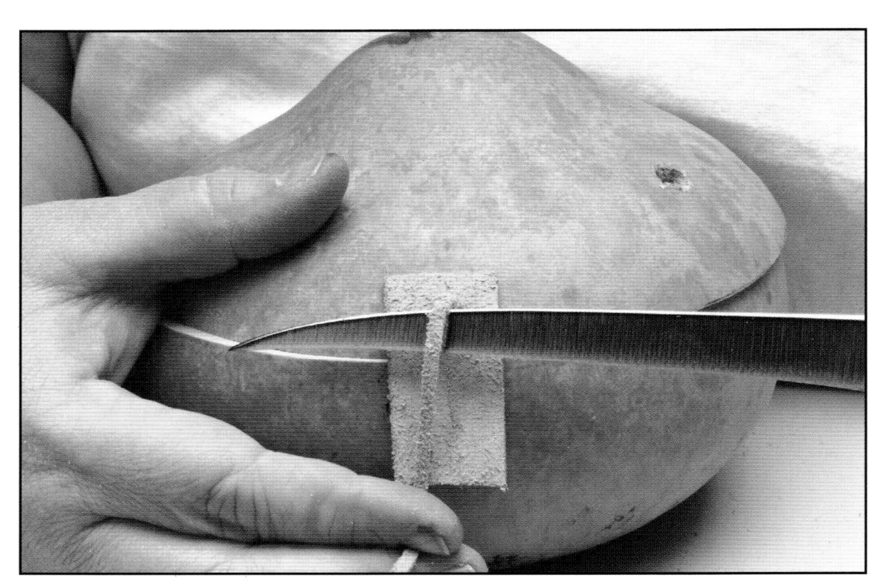

Trim the end.

Bore a hole in the gourd's belly in the middle of the slit mark, using an ice pick. Enlarge this hole with a knife to fit a double thick shoelace.

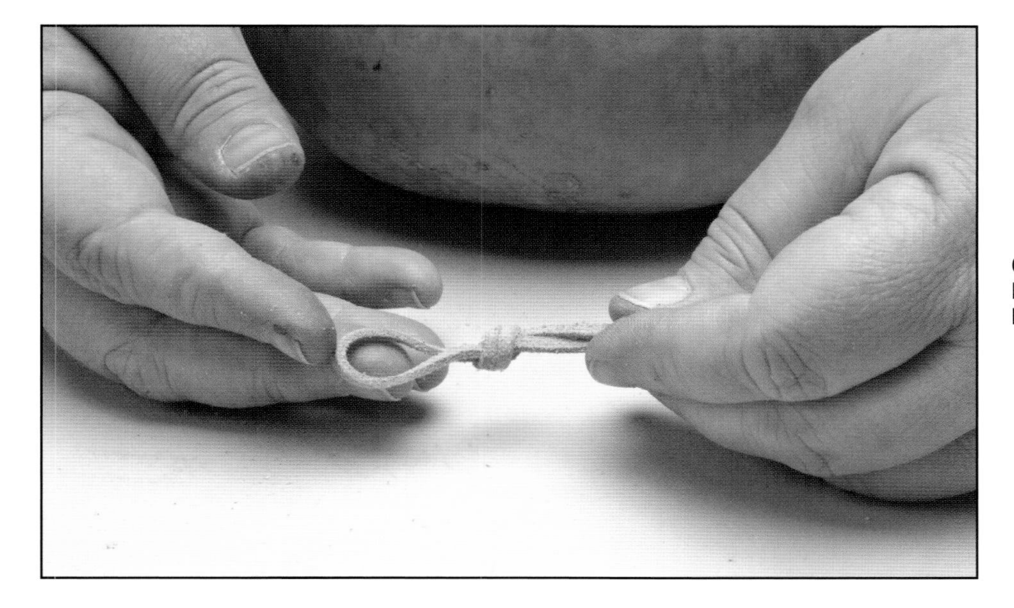

Cut a piece of leather shoelace long enough to double over and knot, making a loop.

From inside the gourd, push the loop end through the hole until the knot catches.

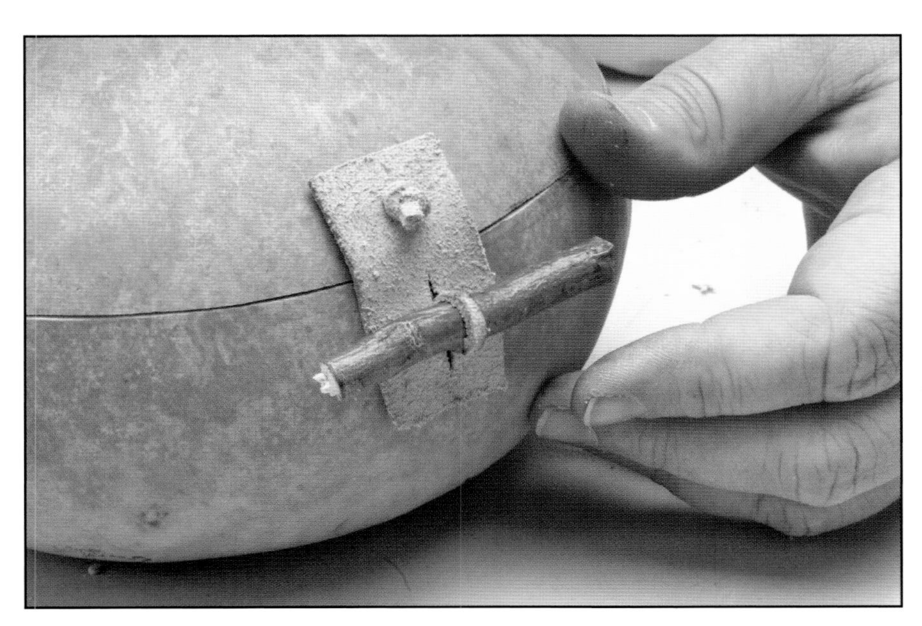

Push the loop through the slit in the latch and hold it in position by inserting a trimmed branch through the loop.

Repeat this procedure for the other two latches.

Vessels

Enough of jars—let's move on to water canteens! Use canteen or bottleneck gourds for water vessels. I have not read any historical articles documenting whether or not our ancestors coated the interior of the gourds used for drinking vessels, but surely no one would have chosen to endure the bitter aftertaste of drinking water stored in an untreated gourd! I can only assume the interiors were coated with some kind of available wax as a barrier, not only to protect the gourd from the constant contact with the fluid, but also to maintain the integrity of the drink. Of course, melting and handling hot wax at demonstrations is dangerous so I usually do the waterproofing part at home and finish the other parts of a water vessel at an event or lecture. This will be the place in this book where I break with 'history' and use an oven and a crock-pot for safety.

Let's get started with a canteen gourd.

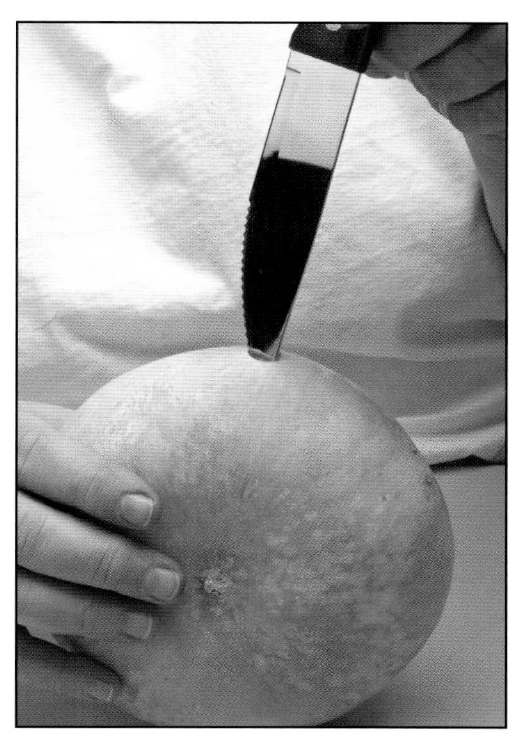

Tip the gourd on its end vertically and use a knife to twist a hole into whichever end you choose to be the top—where the stopper will eventually be.

Choose a canteen gourd, remove the stem if it is still attached, and clean the exterior as we did in the beginning of the book when making the bowls. We're starting here with a clean canteen.

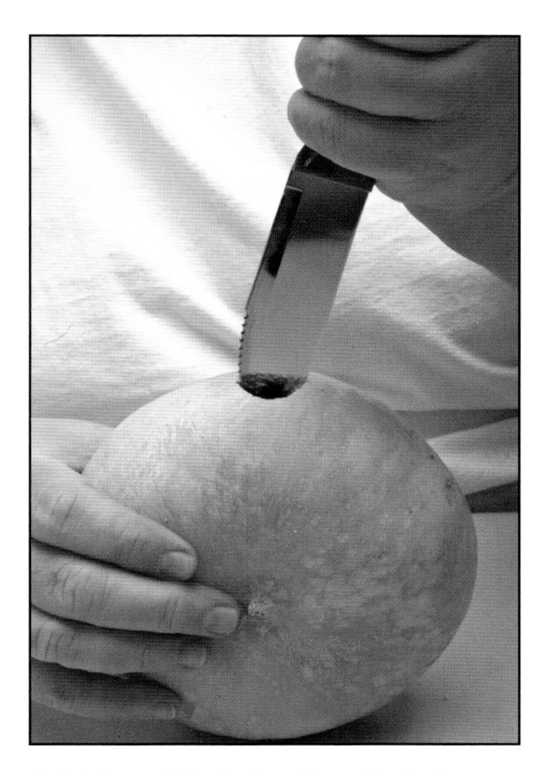

Twist the knife's tip to enlarge the hole until you get an opening large enough to work with as you clean out the interior.

Shake out the loose seeds and pith.

Use a stick and a spoon to scrape out the leftover big pieces. (A spoon can be bent to reach those hard-to-reach areas.) Shake out the debris.

Once the big stuff is out, break up some oyster shells or small stones with a mallet and put several handfuls of sharp bits into the gourd and shake in a circular fashion to abrade other loose stuff away from the interior wall. This will take a while so empty the gourd every once in a while and keep shaking with fresh shards, and on and on.

Eventually it will be obvious nothing more needs to be done because all that falls out is dust.

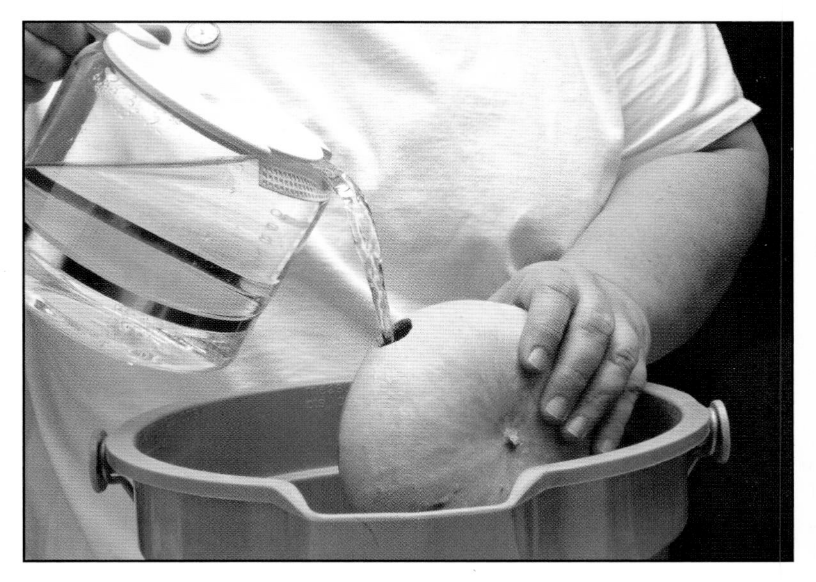

At that point, splash water around the inside to release loose dust particles—and empty. Repeat until the emptied water is clear.

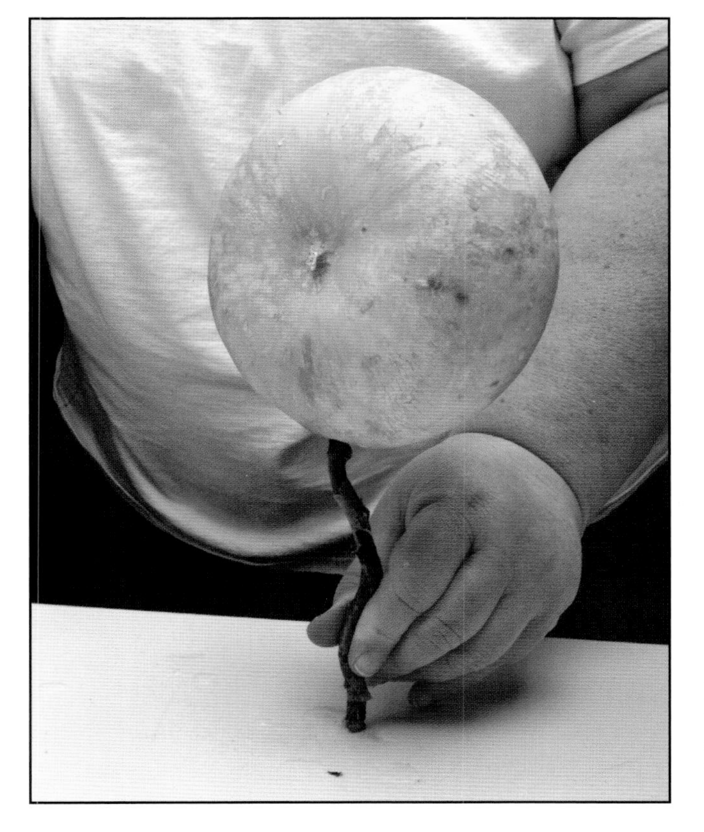

Hang the gourd upside down and let it dry thoroughly; you'll want to occasionally turn it to be sure no drips are settling anywhere. Be generous with the drying time because trapping even the smallest amount of moisture in the wall under a coating of wax will cause it to rot.

Once thoroughly dry, heat the gourd to expand the gourd cells ever so slightly, and make them ready to accept wax between those cells. While warming the gourd in a low-temperature oven – or by letting it sit in direct sunlight on a hot day – liquefy a fairly large chunk of food-grade wax. I do this by sitting a smaller pot inside a crockpot of hot water...a safe double boiler so that stray drips of wax won't come in contact with fire or any electrical element. The goal is to melt the wax, not bring it to a boil.

As soon as the last bit of wax is barely apparent, take the pan out of the crockpot. The existing heat in the melted wax will melt any bits that remain.

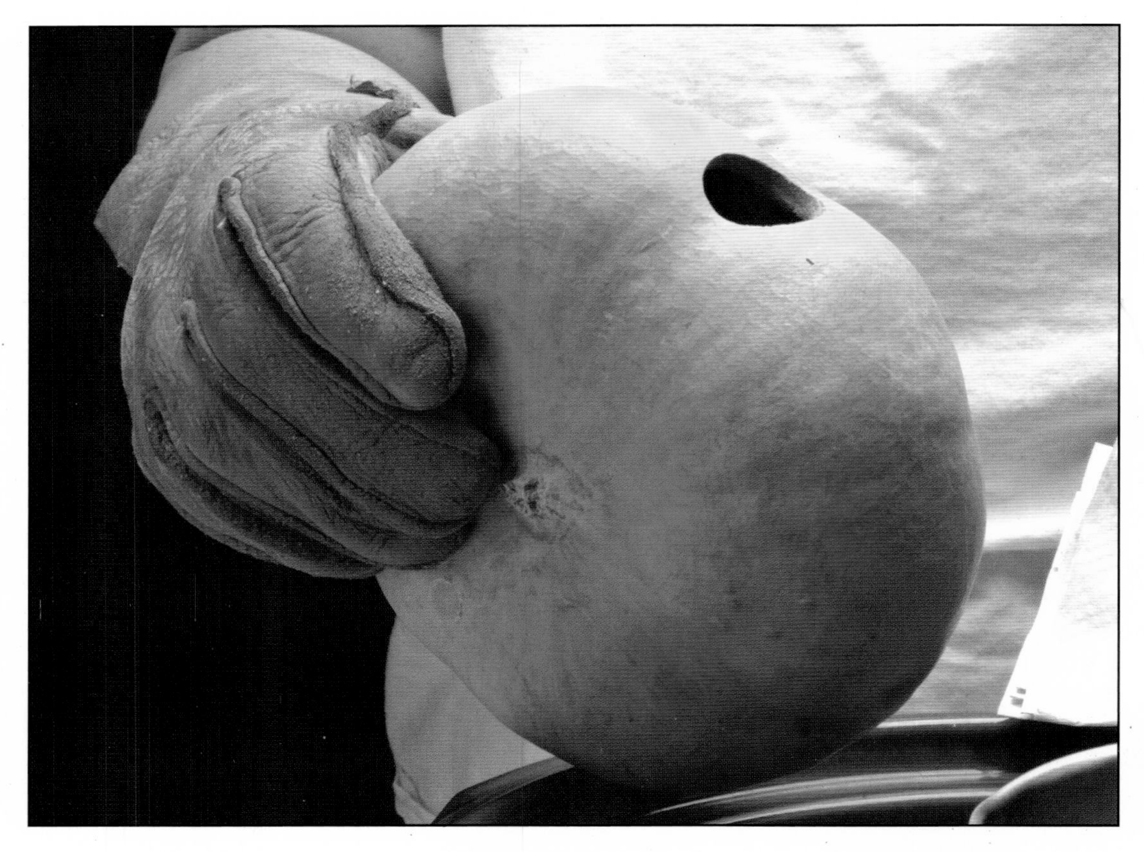

Have a glove or towel ready to hold the warmed gourd as you pour the melted wax into the gourd. (Note: The towel or glove is not necessarily needed to hold the warmed gourd, but rather to hold it after you've poured the melted wax into it because then it will be hot! Melted wax will burn skin, so careful, careful.)

Get a good grip and, working quickly, pour the melted wax into the gourd.

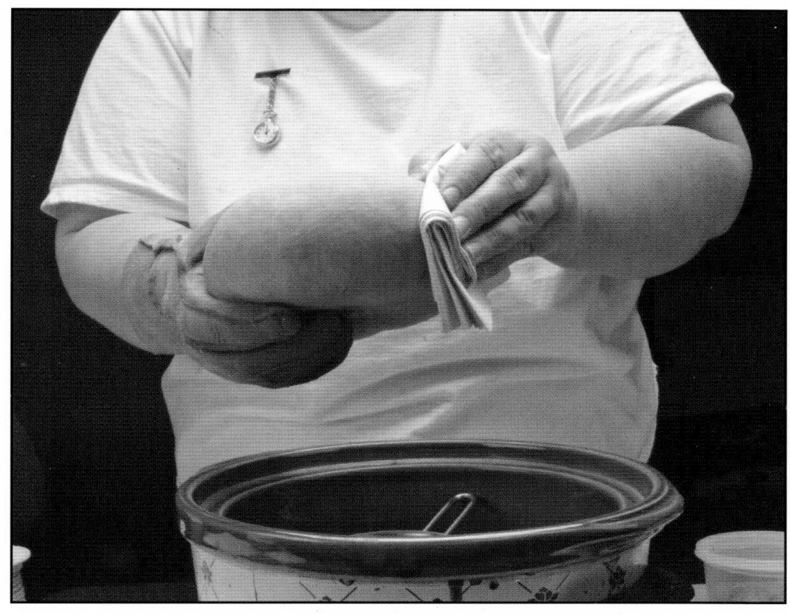

Vigorously swish the wax around the interior a couple of times to coat it thoroughly. Work with common sense and composure, but do not dilly-dally because you do not want the wax to cool and clump up inside the gourd.

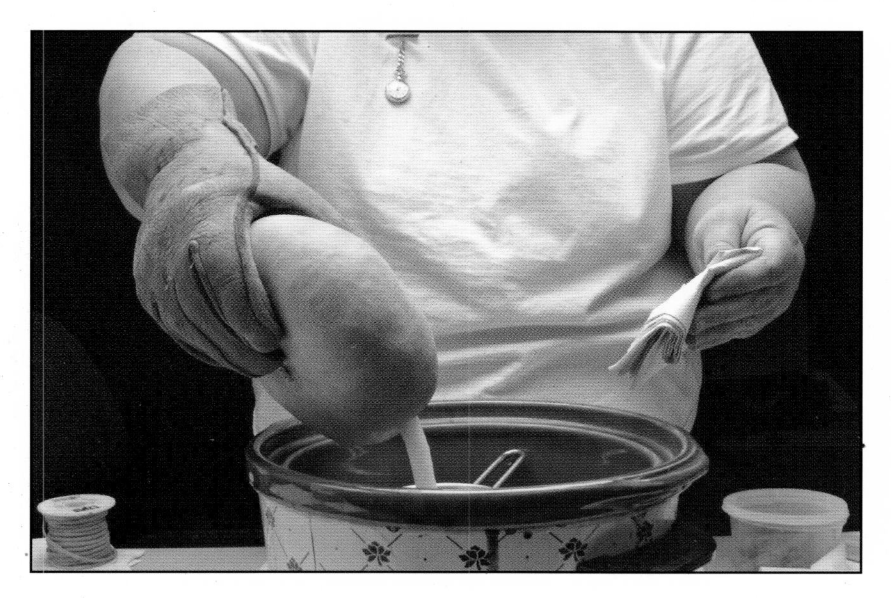

Pour the melted wax back into the pot to reheat, twirling the gourd as you empty so that the lid gets coated too.

A gourd with warm wax will not accept a second coating. Let the gourd cool completely before applying the second coat of wax.

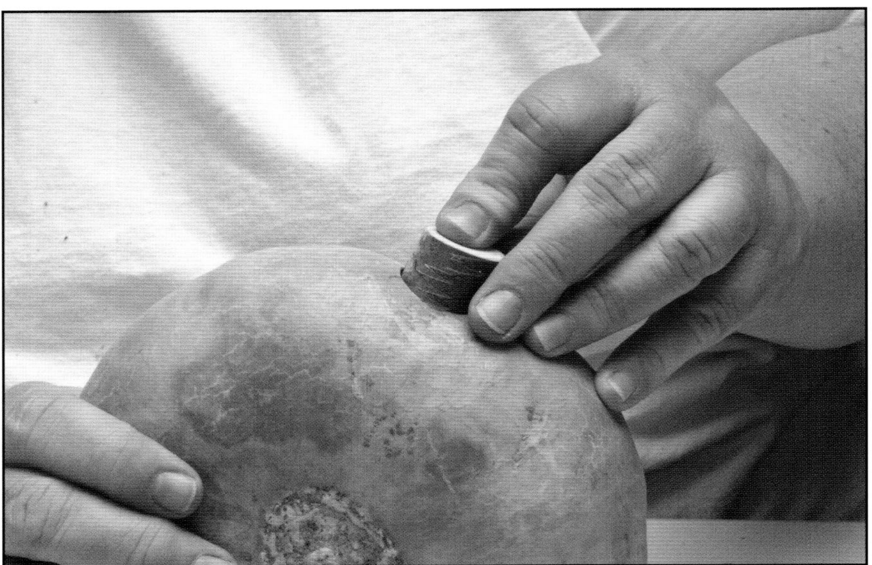

While the gourd is cooling, select a branch with a diameter slightly larger than the entry hole to use as a stopper. Cut it to be about 2-inches in length, take off the bark, and whittle it at a slight angle to fit the hole.

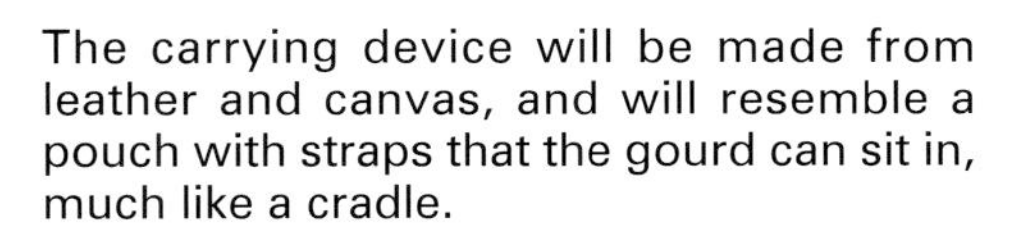

The carrying device will be made from leather and canvas, and will resemble a pouch with straps that the gourd can sit in, much like a cradle.

Cut a piece of tightly woven cloth, like canvas, into a rectangle that is as wide as the diameter of the gourd and twice the diameter of its length.

Fold the cloth in half lengthwise and puncture a hole in each of the corners at the fold with the ice pick, spreading the threads a little.

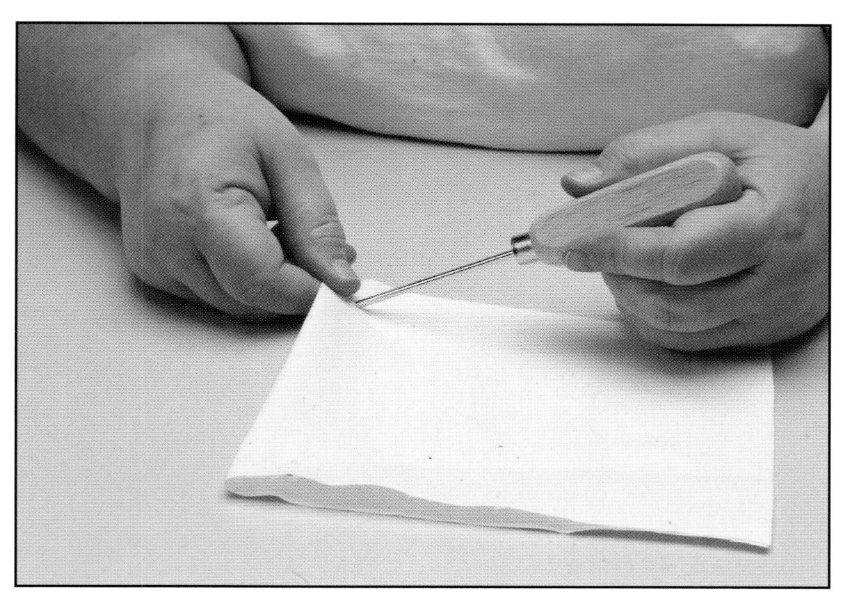

Fold over the ends of the cloth to make a 1-inch hem and puncture a hole in each of the corners, spreading the threads a little.

Get two 5-foot pieces of leather strips — I use shoelaces for this because they come already measured and are made to be sturdy.

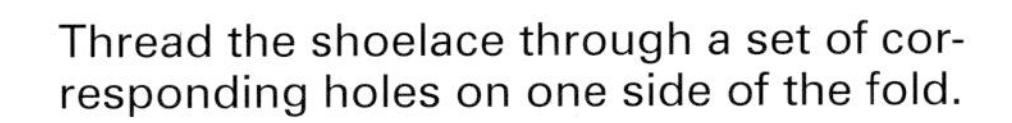

Thread the shoelace through a set of corresponding holes on one side of the fold.

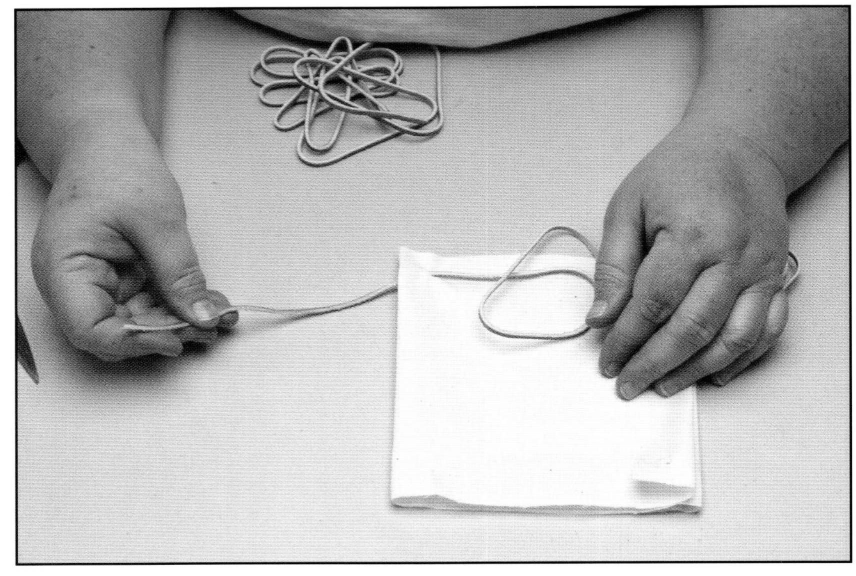

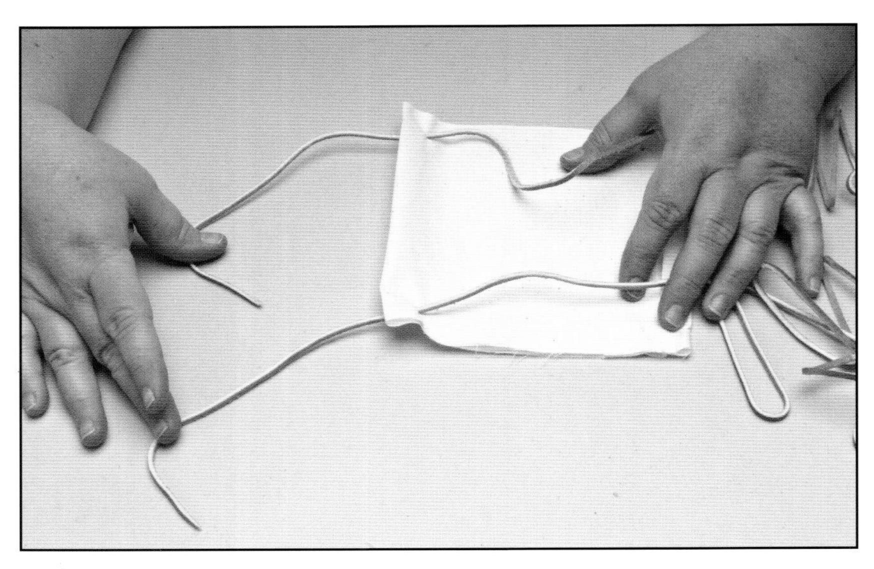

Repeat with the other shoelace through the other set of holes at the fold.

Open the canvas and center it along the length of the shoelaces.

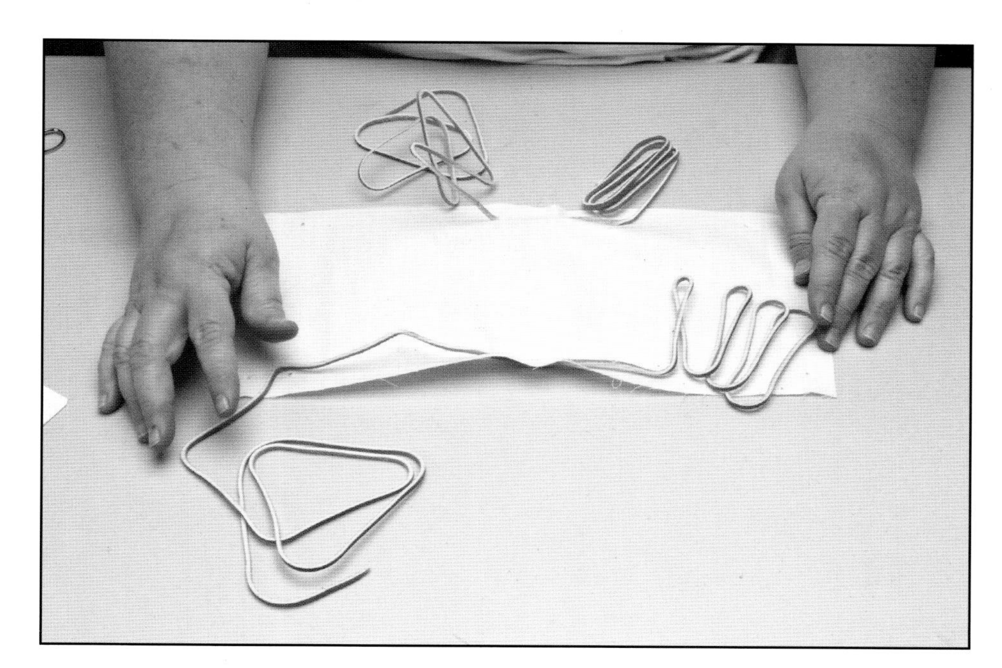

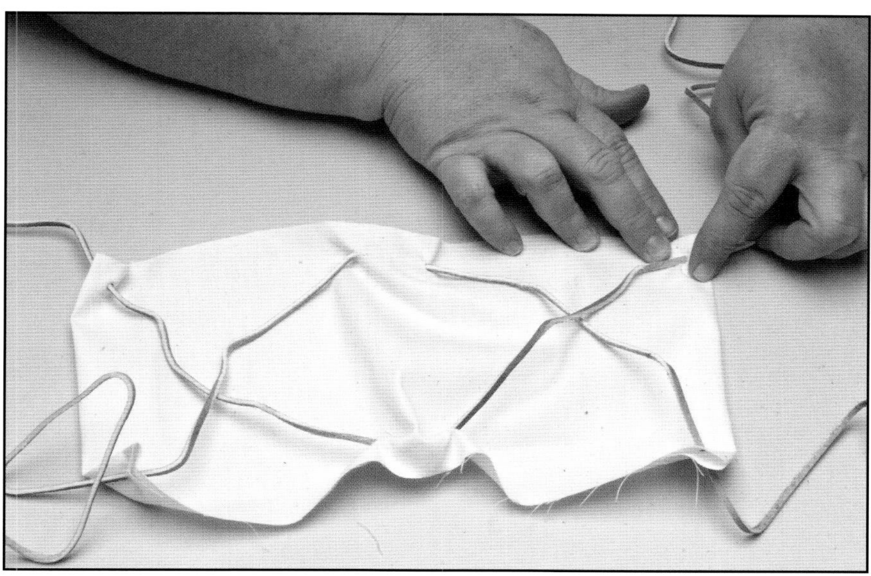

On each side of the canvas fold, cross the shoelaces and thread the ends through the hem holes.

Turn the canvas over and lay the gourd on one side of the fold, positioning the hole at the hem end of the cloth.

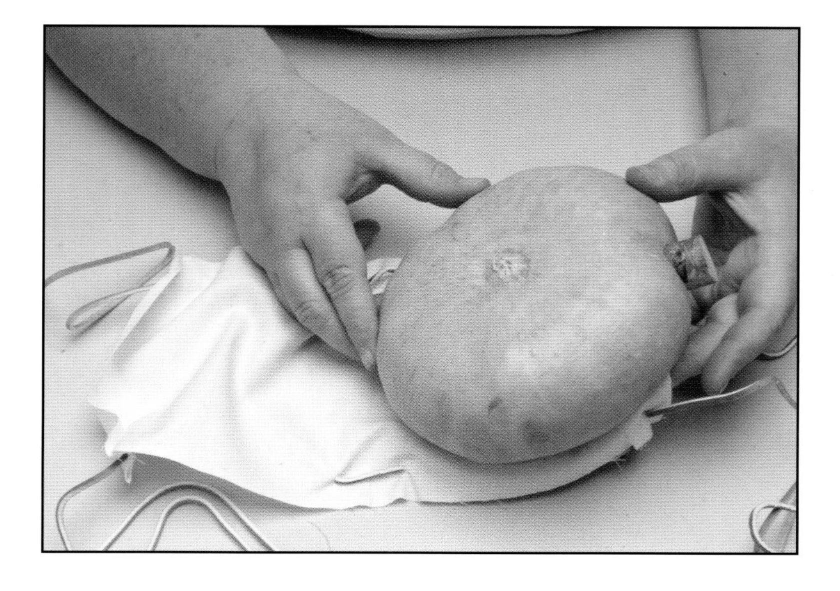

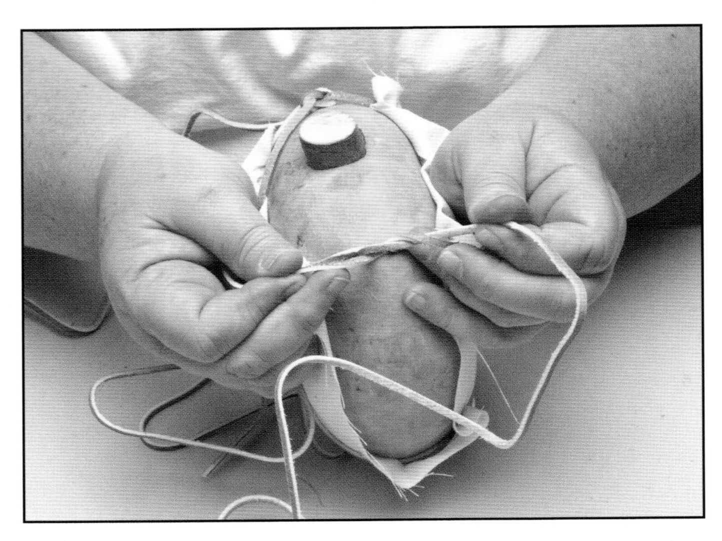

Fold the canvas over the gourd and bring the hems toward each other by pulling the front and back shoelaces tightly into a knot on opposite sides of the drinking hole.

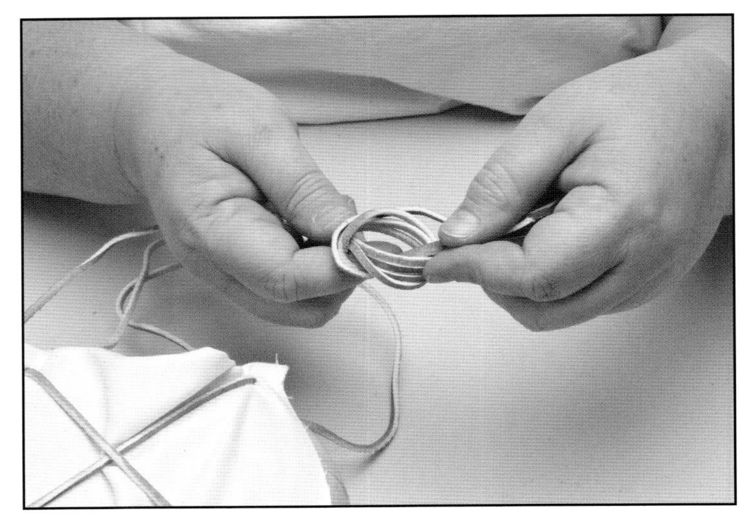

Tie a knot to secure the ends.

There—it should provide you with drinkable water. (Note: Be sure not to leave your gourd in the sun or the wax will re-melt and undo all your efforts.) After using it, rinse it out and hang it upside down to dry. You will have to retreat it eventually, but it should be functional for many outings.

Using a bottleneck gourd to make a drinking vessel is done in much the same way, but has a curve at the neck of the gourd.

Let's move on to bottleneck vessels.

Shake out the loose debris.

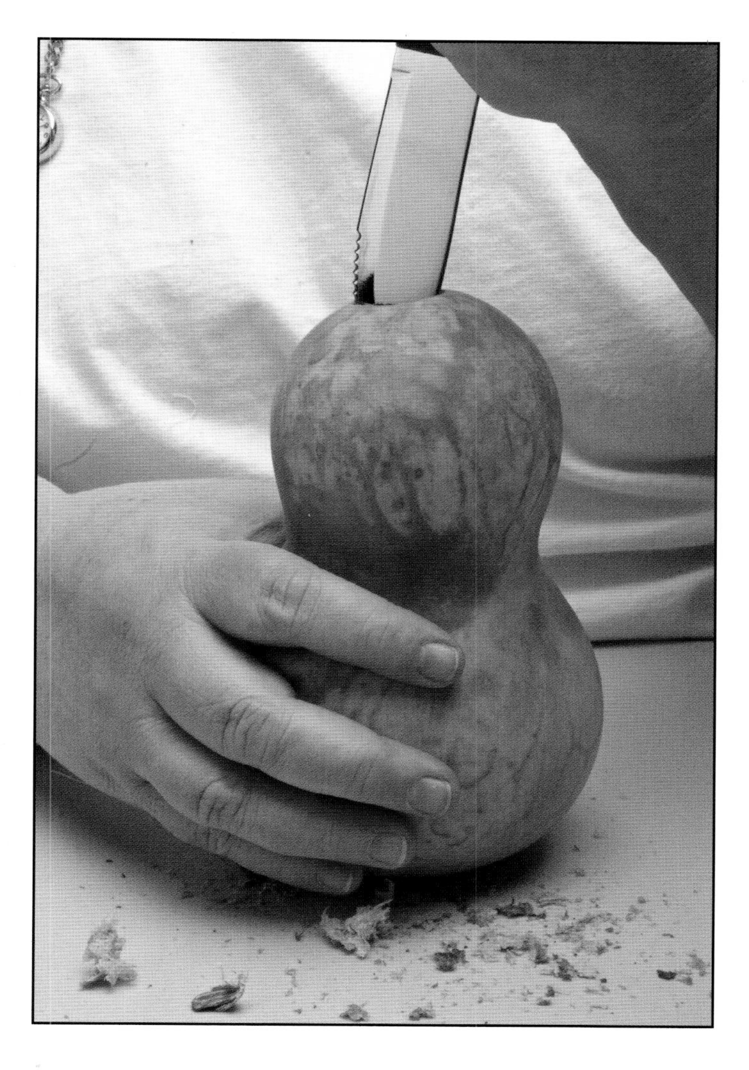

Cut the gourd open at the top, as we did for the canteen gourd.

Use a stick for scraping what large debris you can, using a bent spoon for some of the curved parts.

Proceed with gutting, waterproofing and stopper techniques shown previously with the canteen gourd.

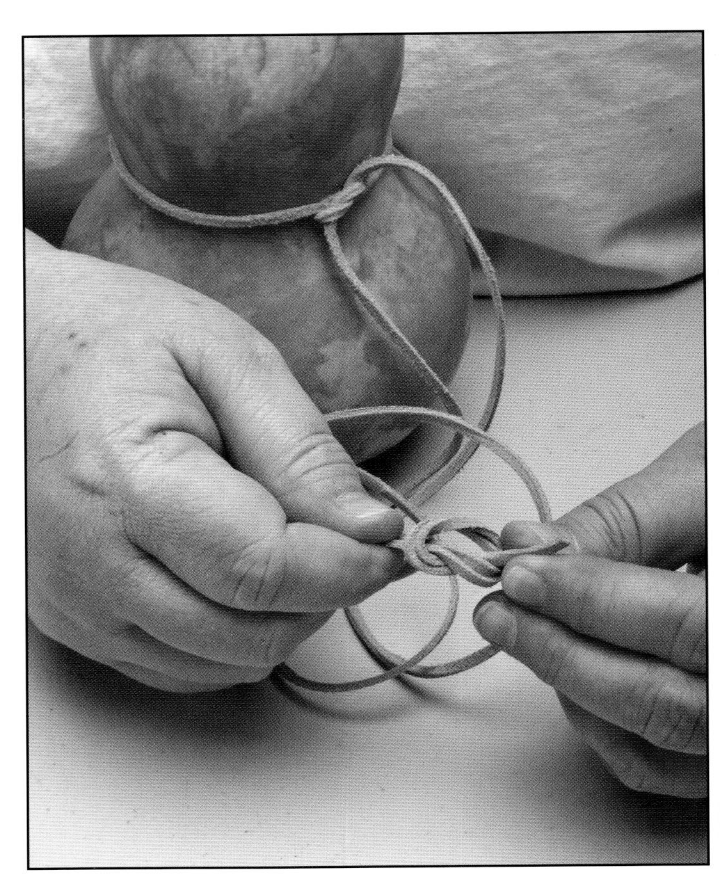

Making a handle or carrying strap for a bottleneck water gourd is as simple as tying a length of leather around the neck and then knotting the ends together.

Using another piece of leather, do the same on the opposite side, tying both ends together.

Part Four:

Making Utensils

Few gourds are more appropriately named than the dipper gourds and spoon gourds. Dippers and spoons look similar: a rounded bowl at the end of a handle. The distinguishing difference, except for the overall size, is the handle's length. Dipper gourds generally have a much longer handle than spoon gourds, making them handy when reaching into a well bucket for a drink of water. Spoons, on the other hand, have shorter handles, smaller bellies, and are more manageable in the kitchen or at the herbalist for getting into jars.

Let's get started with a dipper.

Choose a handled gourd and clean the exterior as we did earlier for the bowls to remove mold and dehydrated skin debris off the surface. We are starting here with a clean gourd.

Lay the gourd down and mark a spot where the gourd belly can be cut just above the line of the handle. It is important to maintain the curve where the handle meets the belly so the bowl does not snap off with use.

Using a knife, scrape an opening in the wall at the spot you marked and insert the blade.

Cut across the belly of the gourd and take off the top.

Scrape out the debris.

Using the broomcorn scrubby, scrape around the bowl to release wall debris and smooth the interior surface.

Use a rough stone to smooth the edge of the gourd.

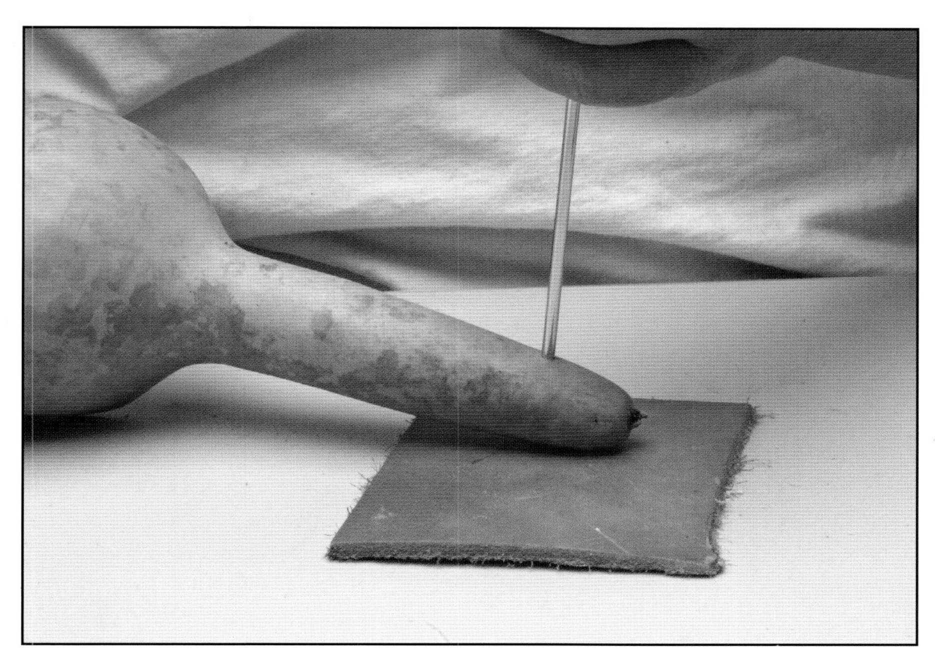

Bore a hole through the handle.

Thread a leather strip through the hole and tie the ends to make a loop for hanging.

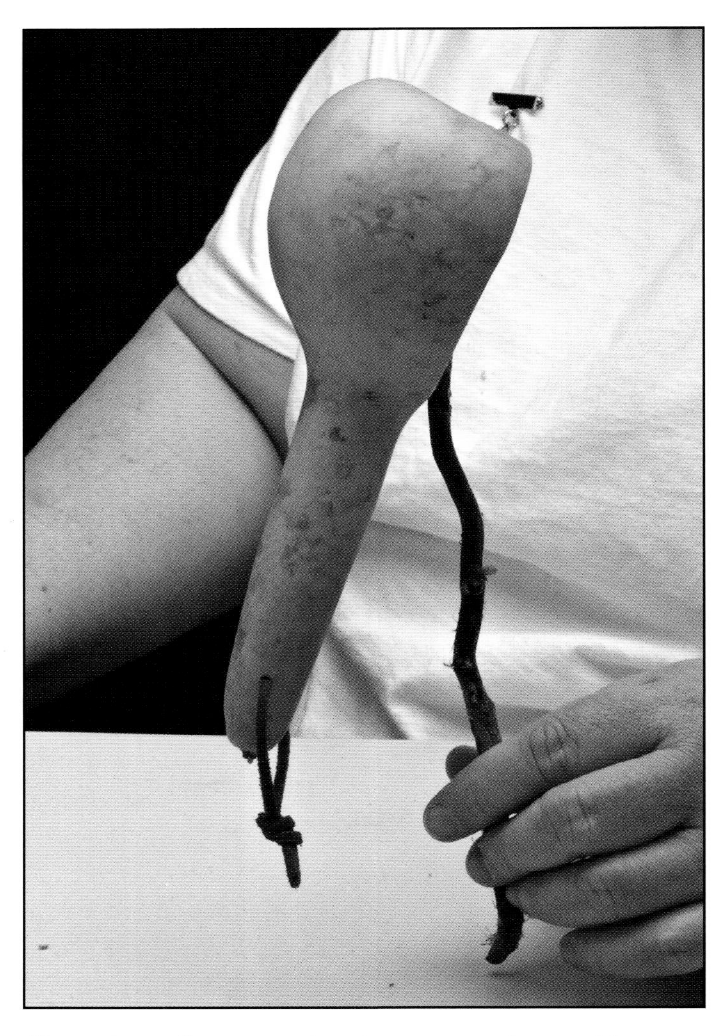

After using a dipper gourd to sip water or stir something, rinse it out and hang it upside down to dry thoroughly. At first, the water may be little bitter, but as the gourd ages you will not notice anything. Unlike canteens and bottle-neck gourds that hold water for periods of time, a quick drink from a dipper gourd does not allow the water to accept the gourd bitterness appreciably.

Using the same technique, turn gourds into all manner of handy everyday devices. Shown is a piece of gourd used as a drip-guard.

Shown is a penguin gourd; it's cut at an angle to be used as a grain scoop.

These spoon gourds were cut in the same way to be used in jars of herbs and spices.

A thick-walled gourd with dozens of holes at the bottom of the belly makes a terrific water sprinkler when dipped in a bucket of water and then passed over plants. Hang it upside down on the fence to dry.

Conclusion

I hope you have learned something useful for your historical or theatrical projects. No doubt I would learn from you when we meet at a festival or event because that is the joy of gourding—information builds and like-minded folks enjoy each other's company and knowledge. Keep researching, keep learning, and keep walking back in time. Not only will you find ways to make and enjoy functional gourds, you walk in the footsteps of our ancestors and perhaps learn something about yourself as well. Visit the many online historical websites that speak about the daily lives of populations in particular periods of time; and, when visiting libraries, keep in mind reference librarians are a fabulous resource.

Also, find your state chapter of the American Gourd Society at www.americangourdsociety.org and ask about any nearby gourd patches. Gourd patches are informal, or sometimes formally structured, subgroups of state AGS chapters and are arranged by county, town, or even neighborhoods depending on the numbers of gourders in the area. They can be a terrific way to connect with others, learn about gourds, and perhaps go to an historical event together–group gourding!

Have a productive day and may the Good Old Gourd be yours!

Angela Mohr
GourdGal

Small banana gourds, cut at an angle, can also be scoops.

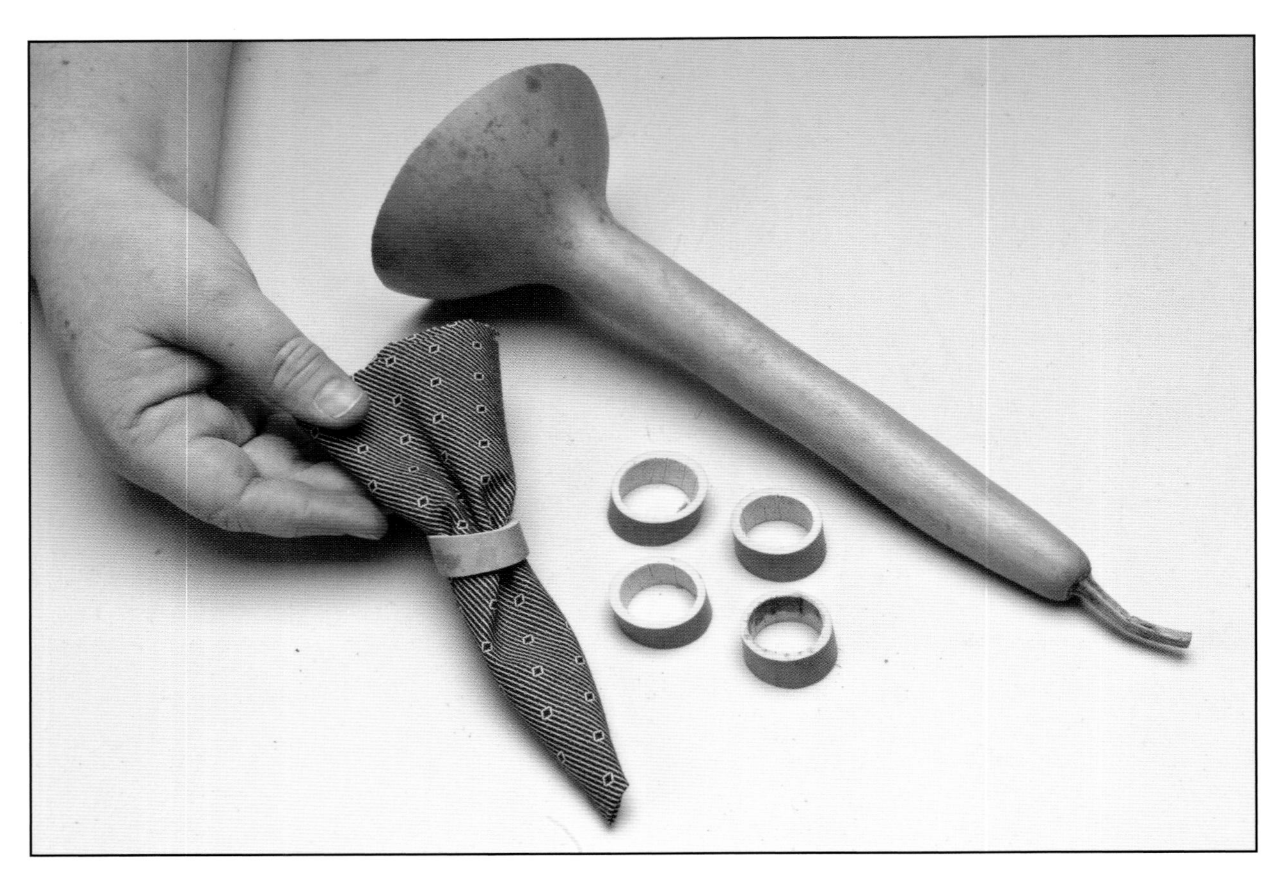

Long gourd handles can be cut-up to make napkin rings.

All gourds, thin or thick, big or little, can be used in some fashion around the house.